The Politics of Precedent on the U.S. Supreme Court

The Politics of Precedent on the U.S. Supreme Court

Thomas G. Hansford
James F. Spriggs II

PRINCETON UNIVERSITY PRESS
PRINCETON AND OXFORD

Copyright © 2006 by Princeton University Press
Requests for permission to reproduce material from this work should be sent to
Permissions, Princeton University Press

Published by Princeton University Press, 41 William Street, Princeton, New Jersey 08540
In the United Kingdom: Princeton University Press, 3 Market Place, Woodstock,
Oxfordshire OX20 1SY

All Rights Reserved

Library of Congress Cataloging-in-Publication Data
Hansford, Thomas G., 1971–
The politics of precedent on the U.S. Supreme Court / Thomas G. Hansford,
James F. Spriggs II.
p.   cm.
Includes bibliographical references and index.
ISBN–13: 978-0-691-12354-7
ISBN–10: 0-691-12354-3 (alk. paper)
1. United States, Supreme Court—Decision making.   2. Stare decisis—United States.
3. Law—United States—Interpretation and construction.   4. Political questions and
judicial power—United States.   I. Spriggs, James F., 1966–   II. Title.

KF8748.H365 2006
347.73'262—dc22   2005047732

British Library Cataloging-in-Publication Data is available

This book has been composed in Sabon

Printed on acid-free paper. ∞

pup.princeton.edu

Printed in the United States of America

10 9 8 7 6 5 4 3 2 1

To my baby girl, Chloe
—Tom

To my grandparents, Willard and Ceola Bock, for their love, generosity, and encouragement
—Jim

Contents

Figures and Tables

TABLES

Acknowledgments

THE DEVELOPMENT OF KNOWLEDGE shares certain similarities with the subject matter of this book, legal change. Both generally develop in an incremental fashion, and the questions they seek to answer are rarely (if ever) articulated in a single text. This project is no exception to this general rule. We began working on it nearly eight years ago, and along the way our understanding of the development of law has developed appreciably. For instance, the origins of chapters 3, 5, and 6 can be found, respectively, in articles we published in *Political Research Quarterly* (2000), *Journal of Politics* (2001), and *Law and Society Review* (2002). The theoretical model that we put forward here, however, differs in fundamental respects from that proposed in those articles. In addition, the research design we employ in chapter 6 is significantly different from its journal article antecedent. Thus, we are hopeful that the following pages provide a fresh look at what we see as an important and exciting topic.

We have benefited from the comments of a host of participants at the various professional conferences at which we have presented this research. Versions of chapter 4 were presented at the 2003 annual meeting of the American Political Science Association, the 2002 annual meeting of the Midwest Political Science Association, the 2002 annual meeting of the Western Political Science Association, and in 2002 at the Arleen Carlson Symposium at the University of Minnesota, Twin Cities. We presented chapter 7 at the 2004 annual meeting of the Southern Political Science Association, the 2004 annual meeting of the Western Political Science Association, and the 2003 annual meeting of the Midwest Political Science Association.

We also owe thanks to numerous colleagues for their advice and suggestions. We especially want to thank Larry Baum, Sara Benesh, Scott Comparato, Lee Epstein, John Gates, Jeff Gill, Virginia Hettinger, Tim Johnson, Brian Sala, John Scott, Don Songer, Harold Spaeth, Paul Wahlbeck, and Chris Zorn. We especially appreciate Saul Brenner's and Jeff Segal's reading of the entire manuscript. We also benefited from comments received when we presented this research at the University of South Carolina and University of California, San Diego. The book further improved as a result of the comments made by the anonymous readers of Princeton University Press. We also thank Chuck Myers, our editor at Princeton, and his staff, especially Jennifer Nippins and Sara Lerner, for helping to bring *The Politics of Precedent* to fruition.

We have had terrific research assistance as we collected our data. This cast includes Dave Damore, Darren DeFrance, Wes Duenow, Larry Eichle, Brian French, Randy Gee, Robin Hastings, Cody Lidge, Chris McCloskey, Alex Mircheff, Danielle Perry, Brandon Reeves, Heather Richards, David Richardson, Elisha Savchak, Jamie Scheidegger, Sarah Schultz, Jim Studt, Chelsea Warner, Danny Williams, and April Wong. Hansford also recognizes and appreciates funding from the University of South Carolina College of Liberal Arts Scholarship Support program; and Spriggs recognizes funding from the Academic Senate of the University of California, Davis and the U. C. Davis Institute of Governmental Affairs.

The Politics of Precedent on the
U.S. Supreme Court

CHAPTER ONE

Introduction

AMONGST OTHER PROTECTIONS, the First Amendment to the U.S. Constitution prohibits Congress from interfering with the right of individuals to assemble in a peaceful manner and speak their mind. The Fourteenth Amendment, the U.S. Supreme Court has determined, requires that the states also respect the freedoms of speech and assembly.[1] General constitutional protections, however, inevitably meet sticky factual circumstances in which there may not be a clear constitutional answer. Can a state's trespassing laws, for example, be used to restrict protest activities on property that is private but generally open to the public? Or, is this sort of activity protected by the First and Fourteenth Amendments?

This question was essentially the one presented to the U.S. Supreme Court in the case *Amalgamated Food Employees Union Local 590 v. Logan Valley Plaza, Inc.* (1968). After union members began picketing a nonunionized supermarket located in a Pennsylvania shopping center, a court granted an injunction prohibiting any union picketing on the grounds of the shopping center. The U.S. Supreme Court held that since the shopping center is generally open and accessible to the public, the First and Fourteenth Amendments prevent Pennsylvania's trespass laws being used to prohibit a peaceful demonstration or picket. Despite the shopping center being private property, the Court concluded that Pennsylvania could not stop the picketers as long as the exercise of their First Amendment rights did not interfere with the ability of others to access the property.

Supreme Court decisions do not just resolve immediate, narrow disputes; they also set broader precedent. The *Logan Valley Plaza* case was no exception, as it established that states, in general, could not restrict speech and assembly on private property if the property is open to the public. Four years after the Court decided *Logan Valley Plaza*, it revisited the precedent when deciding two new cases dealing with protest activity on private, commercial property. In these two decisions, the Court determined that the *Logan Valley Plaza* precedent does not apply to a situation

---

[1] The first applications of the freedom of speech and freedom of assembly protections to the actions of state legislatures occurred in *Gitlow v. New York* (1925) and *DeJonge v. Oregon* (1937), respectively.

in which the private property in question is a stand-alone store (*Central Hardware Co. v. National Labor Relations Board* [1972]) or when the protest activity is unrelated to the private property (*Lloyd Corporation v. Tanner* [1972]).[2] As evidenced by the lower court rulings preceding the Supreme Court's decisions in these cases, it was possible to read the *Logan Valley Plaza* precedent as protecting the rights of the protesters in both situations. Nevertheless, the Court opted to limit the meaning and applicability of *Logan Valley Plaza* in a significant way and thus restrict the reach of the First and Fourteenth Amendments. In fact, the Supreme Court's interpretation of *Logan Valley Plaza* in the *Lloyd Corp.* decision was so critical that in a subsequent decision, *Hudgens v. National Labor Relations Board* (1976), the Court noted that *Lloyd* may have implicitly overruled *Logan Valley Plaza* (424 U.S. 507, 517–18).

The lesson to be drawn from *Logan Valley Plaza* is that Supreme Court precedents do not necessarily remain static over time. Instead, the meaning and scope of a precedent can change as the Supreme Court revisits and interprets it in future cases. Why and when will the U.S. Supreme Court alter the meaning of one of its precedents by negatively interpreting it, as the Court did with *Logan Valley Plaza*? Conversely, when will the Court interpret a precedent positively? By negative interpretation, we mean instances in which the Court chooses to restrict a precedent's reach or call into question its continuing legal validity. Positive interpretation occurs when the Court expressly relies on a case as part of the justification for the outcome of a dispute. This book is not about protest activity and the First and Fourteenth Amendments; it is about one important aspect of legal change at the Supreme Court—the interpretation of Court precedent. We seek to explain when and why the Court develops law through the interpretation of its precedent.

MAKING LAW AND POLICY AT THE U.S. SUPREME COURT

A Supreme Court decision contains two commonly recognized policy outcomes. First, there is the disposition in the case, which determines which litigant prevails in the legal dispute. Second, there is the legal principle announced by the Court that consists of the holding—the answer to the question raised in the case—and the legal reasoning that justifies the holding. The disposition obviously has direct implications for the lit-

---

[2] In *Lloyd*, the Court held that people could not hand out literature opposing the Vietnam War and the draft in a shopping mall. The war and the draft, the Court argued, were not related to the functions of the mall and thus the First Amendment did not protect their activities.

igants' immediate interests in a case. The legal reasoning, however, can have more far-reaching consequences by altering the existing state of legal policy and thus helping to structure the outcomes of future disputes.

Specialists in judicial politics overwhelmingly agree that the essence of the Court's policy-making power resides in its majority opinions (e.g., Epstein and Knight 1998; Epstein and Kobylka 1992; Maltzman, Spriggs, and Wahlbeck 2000, 5–6; Rohde and Spaeth 1976, 172; Segal and Spaeth 2002, 357). These opinions articulate legal principles and, in effect, public policies that affect the behavior of both governmental and nongovernmental decision makers. Court opinions have such effects because they provide information about the possible outcomes of future disputes and signal sanctions for noncompliance (see Spriggs 1996; Wahlbeck 1997). In particular, these legal principles allow decision makers to forecast likely answers to legal questions and thus infer the consequences of their choices (Douglas [1949] 1979; Landes and Posner 1976; Powell 1990). As with policies or institutional rules more generally, Court opinions help actors to overcome uncertainty in their decision-making processes. Put simply, Court opinions create precedents that are relevant for future disputes and thus shape the behavior of forward-thinking actors.

The political science literature, however, manifests a significant disconnect between this common understanding of the importance of law and the state of knowledge regarding how law develops. What is most striking is the paucity of systematic theoretical or empirical studies that treat the law as a variable to be explained. Indeed, only a handful of studies directly seek to explain legal development at the Court, and even they provide somewhat inconsistent and potentially contradictory answers.[3]

Epstein and Kobylka (1992), for example, argue that the most significant variable affecting change in abortion and death penalty policy was the legal arguments put forward by organized interests in the cases, rather than the policy goals of the justices or the surrounding political climate. The overruling of precedent, one study concluded, is largely due to ideological considerations (Brenner and Spaeth 1995). McGuire and MacKuen (2001) suggest the Court's decision to follow a precedent also depends heavily on ideological considerations. And, in his examination of change in search and seizure policy at the Court, Wahlbeck (1997) discovers that

---

[3] By contrast, the legal literature is replete with case studies of particular decisions or areas of the law (e.g., Freed 1996; Kahn 1999; Nalls and Bardos 1991; Schwartz 1996). Although interesting and informative, they manifest two drawbacks that limit their ability to answer the question we pose. First, they are generally descriptive in nature and thus do not present theoretical models of legal development that produce empirically falsifiable predictions. Second, they do not offer rigorous empirical tests of the hypotheses they do propose. See Epstein and King (2002) for a cogent discussion of these issues.

ideological considerations matter, but finds some support for the influence of precedent.

Even recent research focusing on the choices the justices make while crafting opinions does not directly address how law develops. Most notable are studies regarding the assigning of majority opinions (Brenner 1982; Maltzman and Wahlbeck 1996), bargaining and negotiation among the justices (Epstein and Knight 1998; Maltzman, Spriggs, and Wahlbeck 2000), and the justices' joining of opinion coalitions (Brenner and Spaeth 1988; Epstein and Knight 1998; Maltzman, Spriggs, and Wahlbeck 2000; Wahlbeck, Spriggs, and Maltzman 1999). In their recent book, *Crafting Law on the Supreme Court*, Maltzman, Spriggs, and Wahlbeck (2000, 154), for instance, conclude by saying: "Although we present a theoretical and empirical case for the factors that shape judicial behavior, it is important to note that we have not made the final step, explaining the actual content of Court opinions. That task we leave to the future." Indeed, this is a task that nearly all scholars of judicial politics have left for future study.

One reason for the dearth of research treating the law as a dependent variable has been the near-hegemonic status of the attitudinal model of Supreme Court decision making. The arguments underlying this model—namely, that the justices' votes are exclusively a result of their ideological leanings—have led researchers to study the ideological nature of the individual votes of Supreme Court justices or the dispositions of cases, rather than the policy content of majority opinions. Researchers working in this tradition generally argue that the language in Court opinions constitutes post hoc justifications for the outcome preferred by the justices. Thus, they recommend that scholars study "what justices do [i.e., their votes]" rather than "what they say [i.e., their opinions]" (Spaeth 1965, 879). Although attitudinalists recognize that the "opinion of the Court . . . constitutes the core of the Court's policy-making process" (Segal and Spaeth 2002, 357), there continues to be an overwhelming tendency to study the justices' votes.

The second reason that there has been little systematic research in which development of the law is the dependent variable is that it is a difficult concept to measure. For this reason, most research aimed at understanding legal change actually uses the ideological direction of case outcomes as the dependent variable (e.g., Baum 1988; George and Epstein 1992; Segal 1985).

As a result, while existing studies offer tremendous insight into how justices vote on case dispositions, the literature continues to present an underdeveloped theoretical and empirical understanding of why and when law changes. This situation persists in spite of recognition that "analyses of courts ought to center on the law that is established by judicial decisions" (Knight and Epstein 1996, 1021). The goal of this book is to take up this charge and contribute to our understanding of legal change at the U.S. Supreme Court.

Quite obviously, the law is a complex and multifaceted phenomenon that includes a wide variety of components. Epstein and Kobylka (1992, 5) point out this complexity when writing, "The phenomenon of legal change is hydra-headed, comprehending formal judicial actions, executive and legislative behavior, and the behavior of relevant publics. As a result, the concept is subject to definition and observation from a wide variety of perspectives." Even when limiting the concept of law to formal judicial actions, it encompasses the Court's interpretation of federal statutes and treaties, the U.S. Constitution, and the rules announced in previous Court opinions.

As elaborated below, we carve out one element of the law on which to focus—the Court's interpretation of the precedents set by its prior opinions. Given the importance of the Court's precedents as referents for behavior, and the fact that their meaning and scope can change over time, we think they are a good place to begin to analyze how law develops. Our central objective is to provide a systematic theoretical and empirical analysis of the Court's decisions about when and how to interpret existing Court precedents. With this book, we hope to shed light on the Court's most important task, the shaping of legal policy.

THE DEVELOPMENT OF LAW AND THE INTERPRETATION OF PRECEDENT

Political scientists, legal scholars, and practicing lawyers commonly recognize that precedent is one of the central components of the American legal system. By precedent, we mean the legal doctrines, principles, or rules established by prior court opinions. These legal principles indicate the relevance or importance of different factual characteristics for a dispute and set forth legal consequences or tests that attach to particular sets of these factual circumstances (Aldisert 1990; Richards and Kritzer 2002; Schauer 1987). In so doing, precedents convey information that allows decision makers to predict (within certain bounds) the likely legal consequences of different choices and infer the possible range of outcomes of potential disputes.

Importantly, the exact nature of the legal rule established by a Supreme Court opinion can change over time (Epstein and Kobylka 1992; Levi 1949; Wahlbeck 1997). The Court rarely defines doctrine in a comprehensive or complete manner in any one opinion. It sometimes takes a series of opinions to clarify a rule, fill in important details, and define its scope or breadth (Ginsburg 1995, 2124; Landes and Posner 1976, 250). When Court opinions legally treat or interpret an existing precedent they shape it by restricting or broadening its applicability.[4] Legal rules or precedents can thus evolve as the Court interprets them over time.

Broadly speaking, the Court's legal interpretation of precedent takes two forms; and it is these two forms of interpretation on which this book will primarily focus. First, the Court can interpret a precedent positively by relying on it as legal authority (Aldisert 1990; Baum 2001, 142; Freed 1996; Johnson 1985, 1986; McGuire and MacKuen 2001). When doing so, for example, the Court can follow the precedent by indicating that it is controlling or determinative for a dispute. The positive interpretation of precedent thus involves the Court's explicit reliance on the case for at least part of its justification for the outcome in the dispute before it. This treatment of precedent can invigorate its legal authority and possibly expand its scope.

Second, the Court can negatively interpret a precedent by restricting its reach or calling into question its continuing importance. The Court can, for example, distinguish a precedent by finding it inapplicable to a new factual situation, limit a case by restating the legal rule in a narrower fashion, or even overrule a case and declare that it is no longer binding law (see Baum 2001, 142; Gerhardt 1991, 98–109; Johnson 1985, 1986; Maltz 1988, 382–88; Murphy and Pritchett 1979, 491–95). With this kind of interpretation, the Court expresses some level of disagreement with the precedent and, as a result, may undercut the legal authority of a precedent and diminish its applicability to other legal disputes.

The case with which this chapter began, *Logan Valley Plaza*, provides a clear example of a precedent that the Court negatively interpreted. For an illustration of both positive and negative interpretations of Court precedent, in a very different subject area, consider *Warren Trading Post v. Arizona Tax Commission* (1965), where the Court overturned an Arizona statute that taxed a retail trading business operated on an Indian reservation but owned by a non-Indian. The Court ruled that federal law regarding trading on Indian reservations was "all-inclusive" and designed to ensure that "no burden shall be imposed upon Indian traders for trading with Indians on reservations" except as authorized by Congress (380 U.S. 685, 691). The Court argued that the state's tax on gross income in this case would result in such a burden by creating financial hardships for those taxed that would "disturb and disarrange" the federal regulatory scheme (380 U.S. 685, 691). The Court therefore concluded that the state tax was preempted by federal legislation.

---

[4] We use the terms "legal treatment" and "interpretation" synonymously throughout this book.

The Court has on several occasions interpreted or treated this precedent in the context of deciding other disputes. For instance, in *White Mountain Apache Tribe v. Bracker* (1980), the Court scrutinized Arizona's decision to apply license and tax regulations to non-Indian corporations doing business on an Indian reservation. In holding that federal law preempted Arizona's actions, the Court expressly anchored its decision on *Warren Trading Post*: "Both the reasoning and result in this case follow naturally from our unanimous decision in *Warren Trading Post*" (448 U.S. 136, 152). This positive interpretation of *Warren Trading Post* therefore serves to reinforce its ruling. In fact, in their dissenting opinion, Justices Stevens, Stewart, and Rehnquist disagreed with what they saw as an inappropriate extension of this precedent, calling it "disturbing" (448 U.S. 136, 159).

By contrast, in *Moe v. Confederated Salish and Kootenai Tribes of Flathead Reservation* (1976), the Court declared that *Warren Trading Post* did not apply to the question of whether a state could require an Indian trader to collect taxes on items sold to non-Indians. The Indian Tribe argued that *Warren Trading Post* was controlling and led to the conclusion that the taxation scheme at issue intruded on their "freedom from state taxation" (425 U.S. 463, 482). The Court, however, read the precedent more narrowly than the Tribes, saying that because the two taxation schemes differed in substantial ways, *Warren Trading Post* "does not apply" (425 U.S. 463, 482). The Court's distinguishing of *Warren Trading Post* therefore represents a negative interpretation of the precedent.

Most recently, in *Department of Taxation and Finance of New York v. Milhelm Attea and Bros.* (1994), the Court negatively interpreted *Warren Trading Post* and further narrowed its reach. At issue was New York's adoption of regulations that, among other things, limited the quantity of untaxed cigarettes that wholesalers could sell to Indian tribes and tribal retailers. The regulations were adopted to combat the problem of non-Indians purchasing untaxed cigarettes on the reservations. Relying on the legal principle from *Warren Trading Post*, the New York Court of Appeals determined that federal law preempted New York's ability to regulate the activities of the licensed Indian traders. In reversing the lower court's judgment, the Supreme Court wrote that "Although broad language in our opinion in *Warren Trading Post* lends support to a contrary conclusion, we now hold that Indian traders are not wholly immune from state regulation that is reasonably necessary to the assessment or collection of lawful state taxes" (512 U.S. 61, 75). This negative interpretation of *Warren Trading Post* clearly curtails its reach by reading it to say that there is no blanket immunity for Indian traders.

As evident, the precise meaning of the legal principle from *Warren*

Trading Post did not remain static but changed over time as the Court used it in deciding subsequent legal disputes. In each case, the Court revisited the legal principle and interpreted it in ways that had clear implications for its continuing role in structuring future outcomes. The positive or negative interpretations of this precedent therefore helped to shape the law, and in so doing, potentially influenced a state's ability to collect revenue, the relationship between states and tribes, and the relationship between states and the federal government.

The negative interpretation of *Warren Trading Post* in *Milhelm Attea*, for instance, has had real influence in this area of the law. Since this interpretation of the *Warren Trading Post* precedent, lower courts have on at least five occasions explicitly followed *Milhelm Attea* and adopted its view, rather than that put forward in *Warren Trading Post*. As the Court of Appeals for the Tenth Circuit put it (213 F. 3d. 566, 582), *Milhelm Attea* "narrowed its [the Supreme Court's] interpretation of the [Indian] trader statutes." As a result, the Tenth Circuit in this case rejected the Indian Tribes' argument that a Kansas motor fuel tax was illegal because it was preempted by federal law.

This example of *Milhelm Attea*'s effect demonstrates a broader point. Court opinions matter because they help determine societal opportunities and constraints, providing advantages to some actors relative to others. Court opinions are not neutral but serve to redistribute resources in society. By changing the law, the Court can cause distributional consequences in society by helping to structure the outcomes of future disputes and thus affect who wins and loses in society. The Supreme Court's precedents influence the disposition of cases in lower courts (e.g., Comparato and McClurg 2003; Johnson 1987; Songer, Segal, and Cameron 1994; Songer and Sheehan 1990), structure the policy choices of bureaucratic agencies (Spriggs 1996, 1997), influence the issues on which the media focus (Flemming, Bohte, and Wood 1997), affect public opinion (Hoekstra 2000, 2003; Johnson and Martin 1998), and influence the behavior of private parties (e.g., Bond and Johnson 1982; Cooter, Marks, and Mnookin 1982; Priest and Klein 1976). In short, the interpretation of precedent is an important legal and political event that can help structure the future behavior of both governmental and nongovernmental decision makers.

The puzzle arising from this discussion becomes why the Court chose to interpret this precedent when and how it did. Why did the Court, for example, positively interpret *Warren Trading Post* in *Bracker* but negatively treat it in *Moe* and *Milhelm Attea*? More generally, the key theoretical question is the following: Why and when does the Court interpret its precedents positively or negatively? That is the question we take up in this book.

A Brief Account of Existing Answers

Earlier in this chapter, we noted that few systematic studies of the Supreme Court directly focus on the development of the law. Nevertheless, existing research does have something to say about Supreme Court decision making more generally. Here, we briefly review existing theoretical approaches to Court decision making and the limited number of studies that use these approaches to study legal change at the Court. Our goal is to give the reader an overview of the current state of the literature and situate our study accordingly.

Broadly speaking, the literature on Supreme Court decision making is dominated by two competing paradigms (see Clayton and Gillman 1999; Segal and Spaeth 2002). One tradition contends that justices are primarily motivated by concerns about substantive policy outcomes. The attitudinal model, for example, proposes that the justices vote for the liberal or conservative outcome in a case exclusively as a function of their ideological predispositions (Segal and Spaeth 2002). Rational choice explanations predicting that the justices act strategically when deciding cases also start from the premise that judges are policy-oriented decision makers (Epstein and Knight 1998; Maltzman, Spriggs, and Wahlbeck 2000). The common denominator among these scholars is their assumption that justices have one overriding goal—to set legal doctrine that will result in policy outcomes that reflect their preferences.

The second perspective guiding the study of the Court, the legal model, emphasizes that the justices are motivated by a sense of duty or obligation to follow particular legal principles, rights, and norms (e.g., Gillman 1999; Kahn 1999; Wechsler 1959). In contrast to the prior approach, this viewpoint contends that judges seek to adhere to these rules or norms irrespective of the substantive policy outcomes that will result from their application. Scholars in this tradition argue, for example, that judges strive to adhere to precedent (e.g., Dworkin 1978) or decide cases consistent with certain conceptions of rights or theories of constitutional interpretation (Kahn 1999), such as the Founders' notion of appropriate policy making (Gillman 1993). In short, this perspective contends that judges are jurisprudentially oriented decision makers who respond to normatively relevant legal factors.

One of the central debates in the social scientific study of the Court today is whether Supreme Court justices are motivated by law or policy. A series of recent books (Clayton and Gillman 1999; Segal and Spaeth 2002; Spaeth and Segal 1999) and journal articles (Brenner and Stier 1996; Segal and Spaeth 1996; Songer and Lindquist 1996) seeks to defend one of these two positions. While many (if not most) scholars recognize that the justices probably respond to both of these concerns (e.g., Baum 1997), the literature nonetheless tends to present them as competing explanations. According to Segal and Spaeth's (2002, 53) recent treatise on the attitudinal model, for example, "the legal model and its components serve only to rationalize the Court's decisions and to cloak the reality of the Court's decision making process." Kahn (1999, 197), by contrast, concludes that the legal model is "a more credible and useful" approach than a policy-based model. One contribution we make in this book is to show that policy goals and legal concerns are not competing explanations but are inextricably linked to one another as the Court interprets precedent.

When turning to existing research on the interpretation of precedent and legal change, we see that it tends to put forward hypotheses drawn from one or both of these two traditions. First, many studies suggest that the interpretation of precedent depends at least in part on the justices' policy goals (e.g., Brenner and Spaeth 1995; Johnson 1986, 1987; McGuire and MacKuen 2001; Spriggs and Hansford 2001, 2002).[5] When taken together, these studies offer some support for the influence of the justices' ideological points of view, but their results differ from one another in some important respects. Johnson (1986), for instance, concludes that ideological considerations did not influence how the Court interpreted the precedents in his study. Epstein and Kobylka (1992) conclude that ideology played little role in the Court's interpretation of precedent in the area of abortion rights and the death penalty. Wahlbeck (1997) and Brenner and Spaeth (1995) find, however, that ideological considerations matter, respectively, in change in search and seizure policy at the Court and the justices' decisions to overrule precedent. Additionally, McGuire and MacKuen (2001) present data showing that the ideological distance between the Court and a precedent influences the positive interpretation of precedent.[6]

These studies share a common problem that may in part account for their discrepant results: they put forward the hypothesis of ideological

[5] Studies of lower federal court responsiveness to the Supreme Court put forward similar claims (see Benesh 2002; Benesh and Reddick 2002; Klein 2002; Songer, Segal, and Cameron 1994).

[6] There is also a literature on the citation of court opinions and patterns of citations across courts. Although these articles are interesting, most of them provide limited leverage for this book because their theoretical focus is not on legal development or the interpretation of precedent. First, many of them are interested in the influence of particular judges, measured by the number of citations to a judge's prior opinions, rather than in how law changes (e.g., Kosma 1998; Landes, Lessig, and Solimine 1998; Merryman 1954, 1977). Second, studies examining patterns of citations across courts have been mainly interested in how characteristics of the courts (e.g., geographical location or size of caseload) or particular judges (e.g., expertise or reputation) affect citations (e.g., Caldeira 1985, 1988; Harris 1985).

influence without considering how it fits into a more general theory of the development of law. Indeed the conjecture of ideological voting principally derives from the attitudinal model, which, as its leading proponents make clear, does not apply beyond the justices' final votes on the merits (i.e., the choice to affirm or reverse the lower court decision) (Segal and Spaeth 2002, 96). Thus, while the hypothesis that legal change is a function of the ideological motives of the justices makes intuitive sense (and certainly plays a role in this process), absent a model of the interpretation of precedent its exact role remains underspecified.

Second, scholars have invoked legal norms as representing one element in the development of law (e.g., Johnson 1985, 1986; McGuire and MacKuen 2001). In so doing, they draw on the legal model of judicial decision making. Again, this perspective seeks to explain Court decisions as a function of legally relevant concerns, such as the factual characteristics of cases and the state of the law as embodied in statutes, the U.S. Constitution, and precedent. Existing accounts provide preliminary support for a relationship between legal variables and the development of the law. For example, studies indicate that the nature of the Court's prior interpretation of a precedent (Spriggs and Hansford 2001, 2002; Ulmer 1959; Wahlbeck 1997), the need to legitimize policy choices (Walsh 1997), and the legal arguments put forward by organized interests (Epstein and Kobylka 1992) influence the law.[7] We emphasize the word "preliminary" because many of these studies conclude that their evidence for these effects is somewhat mixed (see McGuire and MacKuen 2001; Spriggs and Hansford 2002; Wahlbeck 1997) or underwhelming to nonexistent (Segal and Spaeth 2002; Spaeth and Segal 1999).

The hypotheses drawn from the legal tradition have also been put forward without fitting them into a model of the interpretation of precedent or legal change. In addition, many studies of the influence of precedent (e.g., McGuire and MacKuen 2001; Richards and Kritzer 2002; Spriggs and Hansford 2001; Wahlbeck 1997) are susceptible to the criticism that their results are spurious, resulting from the endogeneity of precedent. That is, if one shows that the Court's prior behavior is correlated with its

---

[7] There are two other sources of possible evidence on this point. First, research indicates that the outcomes of cases at various courts depend in part on factual circumstances of the cases (see Richards and Kritzer 2002; Segal 1984; Traut and Emmert 1998). Second, research demonstrates that lower courts tend to be responsive to higher courts (e.g., Pacelle and Baum 1992; Songer and Sheehan 1990; Traut and Emmert 1998; Wahlbeck 1998); and their responsiveness varies according to legal considerations (Johnson 1987; Klein 2002), such as the factual characteristics (Benesh 2002; Songer, Segal, and Cameron 1994) and nonfactual attributes (e.g., the age, ambiguity, and complexity) of a precedent (Benesh and Reddick 2002; Comparato and McClurg 2003).

current behavior, it might not be clear whether this effect is causal (i.e., the prior behavior actually influences the current behavior) or spurious (i.e., the same set of unobserved and unmeasured forces that influence prior Court behavior influence the current Court). As a result, it remains unclear whether and how legal norms enter into this aspect of Court decision making. We agree with Epstein and Kobylka's (1992, 302) assertion that "The law and the legal arguments grounded in law matter, and they matter dearly." But, we contend that the way in which legally relevant considerations matter remains something of a mystery.

Taken as a whole, the literature suggests that the justices' policy goals and legal norms influence the development of law at the Court.[8] We agree that these are the most important variables influencing legal development. Existing treatments of them, however, do not well specify the role they play in this process. In particular, we submit that in order to understand this important aspect of Court decision making, it is necessary to rethink how both the justices' policy preferences and the law help shape legal development. Only by embedding them into a general model of the interpretation of precedent can we understand how they help produce this particular form of legal change.

To address this significant gap in our understanding of the Court, we make two principal contributions to the literature. First, we develop a parsimonious theoretical model that lays bare the essential variables influencing the Court's decision to interpret precedent positively or negatively. To preview, we argue that the justices have two primary reasons to interpret precedent: (1) the justices treat precedent in order to maximize the extent to which the Court's body of precedent reflects their own policy preferences; and (2) the justices use precedent in an effort to legitimize their current policy choices and thus foster the influence of their opinions. We contend that both of these motivations relate to the justices' overriding desire to affect distributional consequences—such as the relative bargaining advantage of different actors and the distribution of resources in society—in ways they prefer.

By elaborating how these two goals combine to influence the Court's choices, we offer a new way of thinking about their role in Supreme Court decision making. Much of the literature asserts (at least

---

[8] Scholars sometimes suggest that aspects of the litigation or political environment, such as the resources or experience of litigants and counsel or the preference of elected political decision makers, may influence the law (e.g., George and Epstein 1992). For example, Wahlbeck (1997) shows that change in search and seizure policy at the Court depended in part on the level of experience of the counsel arguing the case, the presence of amici curiae, and the preferences of the president. Spriggs and Hansford (2001), however, demonstrate that the president and Congress apparently have no influence on the overruling of precedent.

implicitly) that precedent acts either as a constraint that operates across the board (e.g., Knight and Epstein 1996; Wahlbeck 1997) or as a "cloak" that never actually influences the Court (Segal and Spaeth 1993, 2002; Spaeth and Segal 1999). By contrast, we argue that while precedent can operate as a constraint on the justices' decisions, it also represents an opportunity. It represents a constraint in that justices may respond to the need to legitimize their policy choices and thus gravitate toward some precedents rather than others. It represents an opportunity in the sense the justices can utilize precedent to constrain other actors, thereby promoting the outcomes they prefer. By specifying the benefits the justices receive from interpreting precedent positively or negatively based on both the desire to make existing precedent compatible with their policy preferences and their need to justify and legitimize their holdings, we gain a better handle on how these variables influence the Court. As will become clear, our theoretical model also helps to overcome the problem of the potential endogeneity of precedent, allowing us to develop a much clearer test of the causal force of precedent.

The second contribution of this book is empirical in nature. We endeavor to offer rigorous tests of our model's predictions and thus provide a substantive understanding of how our theoretical variables of interest affect the Court's treatment of precedent. We examine how, through 2001, the Court positively or negatively interpreted all of the precedents set by the orally argued cases decided between the Court's 1946 and 1999 terms. By focusing on a large number of cases (6,363) over a considerable period of time (56 years), we can provide an understanding of systematic influences leading to variation in the presence and timing of the Court's interpretations of its precedents. This research design stands in contrast to most social scientific work on this question, which exclusively analyzes particular issue areas (e.g., Epstein and Kobylka 1992; McGuire and MacKuen 2001; Wahlbeck 1997), a small number of cases (e.g., Johnson 1985, 1986), or sensational but infrequent forms of interpretation such as the overruling of precedent (e.g., Brenner and Spaeth 1995; Spriggs and Hansford 2001).

Outline of the Book

In the following pages, we seek to provide answers to the main question posed above—why and when does the U.S. Supreme Court interpret its precedents positively or negatively? Chapter 2 sets forth the theoretical model we use to explain the Court's interpretation of precedent. In chapter 3, we define in detail the manner in which we measure the interpretation of precedent, as well as present descriptive data on its frequency and timing. In chapters 4 through 6, we provide empirical tests of the predictions from our theoretical model. In chapter 4, we specifically examine why and when the Court subsequently interprets a precedent either positively or negatively in the years following the creation of the precedent. In chapter 5 our focus turns to explaining the most dramatic form of negative legal treatment, the Court's overruling of a precedent. Chapter 6 shifts the unit of analysis used in chapters 4 and 5, as we ask how, in a given case, the Court legally interprets existing precedent. That is, while in chapters 4 and 5 the focus is on the precedent, the focus in chapter 6 is on the case that interprets the precedent. Chapter 7 tests empirically our underlying assumption that the Court's interpretation of precedent has meaningful consequences by examining how lower federal courts respond to the Supreme Court's interpretation of its own precedents. Finally, in chapter 8 we review our theory and empirical results and discuss their implications for Supreme Court decision making.

Before moving on, we want to be clear about the scope of this study and the breadth of the conclusions we can draw from it. First, we do not suggest that, either theoretically or empirically, we will provide *the* answer to how law develops. As already indicated, the concept of legal change is broad and multidimensional, and no single study of it can do justice to its full richness and complexity. We therefore chose to focus on a phenomenon that scholars commonly recognize as constituting one important aspect of the law, the interpretation of precedent. This focus, we contend, is a good starting point for understanding legal development, but it most certainly does not capture all of its aspects.

Second, we do not suggest that our empirical focus on the positive or negative treatment of precedent is the only way to examine how their meaning changes over time. We chose these indicators for two principal reasons. They capture in broad terms how the Court does in fact treat its prior opinions and thus provide a nice starting point for addressing this issue. We also chose this conceptualization of interpretation to enhance the reliability of our measures of it. As chapter 3 makes clear, the coding protocols used to generate these dependent variables are replicable and valid and thus meet a necessary requirement for good social science.

We are, however, cognizant of their potential to mask some variation in the treatment of precedent. Some will therefore criticize these measures because they do not tap explicitly the precise way in which the meaning of a precedent changes with each successive interpretation. To capture completely such nuances, one would need to use case studies (e.g., Epstein and Kobylka 1992; Kahn 1999; Nalls and Bardos 1991), which usually limit one's ability to generalize results. We wish to draw broad generalizations and therefore choose to test our theory on a wide range of Court precedents decided over a considerable length of time.

We thus trade off the ability to capture nuances in the content of law as it changes over time for the ability to test rigorously the predictions from our theoretical model.

Third, we wish to be clear that our goal is *not* to test whether Supreme Court justices change their votes due to the norm of *stare decisis* (the norm requiring adherence to precedent), which has been a dominant focus among studies of precedent in recent years (see Brenner and Stier 1996; Lim 2000; Segal and Spaeth 1996; Songer and Lindquist 1996; Spaeth and Segal 1999). Those analyses have most certainly helped us to understand the question of whether precedent leads justices to cast votes they otherwise would not. However, we contend that when one's focus turns to the interpretation of precedent, it is necessary to adopt a different point of view that does not see precedent merely as a constraint. This is not to say that these other studies are asking the wrong question with regard to votes. Rather, we merely point out that our substantive focus and theoretical model lead us to ask a different question.

With these caveats and clarifications in mind, we are hopeful that this study does what all good social science strives to do—articulate a well-defined, parsimonious theory and subject its predictions to rigorous empirical analyses. With this book, we strive to come one step closer to answering the most important question facing judicial scholars: What explains the development of the law?

CHAPTER TWO

Explaining the Interpretation of Precedent

THE SUPREME COURT'S INTERPRETATION or treatment of precedent takes two broad forms. The Court can interpret a precedent positively by relying on it as legal authority, broadening its reach or at least reiterating its continuing legal relevance. The Court can indicate, for example, that a precedent is controlling or determinative for a type of dispute (Aldisert 1990; Baum 2001, 142; Freed 1996). Second, the Court can negatively interpret a precedent by restricting or perhaps eliminating its reach. The Court can, for instance, distinguish a precedent by finding it inapplicable to a new factual scenario or limit a precedent by restating the legal rule in a more restrictive way (see Gerhardt 1991, 98–109; Maltz 1988, 382–88; Murphy and Pritchett 1979, 491–95). Positive and negative interpretations of precedent are thus important, as they directly shape the law. While in chapter 1 we provided specific examples of the way several Supreme Court precedents have been interpreted over time, our ultimate goal is to develop a general explanation for when, why, and how the Court will interpret its precedents. In this chapter, we take an important step towards this goal by developing a theoretical argument explaining the interpretation of precedent. This theoretical argument will then guide the subsequent empirical chapters.

We base our argument on two premises. First, justices interpret precedent to influence the current state of legal policy (Brenner and Spaeth 1995; Epstein and Kobylka 1992; Johnson 1986; McGuire and Mac-Kuen 2001; Wahlbeck 1997). By interpreting precedent, the Court can alter the scope and authority of existing legal rules and thereby influence how other decision makers view and implement these rules. The Court's interpretation of precedent can influence lower court judges and a wide variety of nonjudicial actors, including both policy implementers and potential litigants. Thus, by interpreting precedent and changing the existing legal status quo in the process, the Court can help structure future outcomes.

Second, Supreme Court justices interpret precedent to justify the new policies established in their current opinions (Friedman et al. 1981; Johnson 1987; Walsh 1997). The American public, especially its attentive members and those charged with implementing, enforcing, and interpreting Court decisions, expects the Court to base its decisions on legally relevant criteria. Most notably, the norm of *stare decisis* instructs courts to follow the legal principles articulated in previously decided cases. While legal authority comes in a variety of forms—such as abstract rights principles or modes of interpretation (e.g., original intent) (see Gates and Phelps 1996; Murphy, Fleming, and Barber 1995)—one of the most pervasive (and arguably persuasive) arguments used in Court opinions involve appeals to precedent (Knight and Epstein 1996; Phelps and Gates 1991). *Stare decisis* therefore provides justices with an incentive to link current policy choices to those from the past.

We begin this chapter with a discussion of the importance of policy preferences and precedent in Supreme Court decision making. From this discussion, we develop two motivations driving the Court's interpretation of precedent. Next, we outline the manner in which these two motivations combine to determine the benefit the justices receive from positively or negatively interpreting a precedent. Based on this theoretical framework, we derive the general propositions which will ultimately yield the specific hypotheses tested in subsequent chapters.

The Role of Policy Preferences

Research consistently indicates that the justices' policy preferences are the primary determinant of their votes on the merits of cases (Pritchett 1948; Rohde and Spaeth 1976; Segal and Spaeth 1993, 2002). Perhaps more importantly, evidence also indicates that the justices' policy goals affect other choices they make while on the bench, such as voting on certiorari (Boucher and Segal 1995; Caldeira, Wright, and Zorn 1999), asking questions at oral argument (Johnson 2004), assigning opinions (Brenner 1982; Maltzman and Wahlbeck 1996; Rohde 1972), and joining opinion coalitions (Brenner and Spaeth 1988; Maltzman, Spriggs, and Wahlbeck 2000; Wahlbeck, Spriggs, and Maltzman 1999; Ulmer 1970). Recent research also shows that the bargaining and negotiation that takes place on the Court is largely oriented towards influencing the policy content of majority opinions (Epstein and Knight 1998; Maltzman, Spriggs, and Wahlbeck 2000).

It is important to note, however, that Supreme Court justices do not merely seek to hand down decisions and set precedents that are consistent with their policy preferences. Instead, they endeavor to create legal policy that will actually influence legal and extralegal outcomes in the intended manner. Justice Vinson (1949, 552) suggested as much when he wrote: "What the Court is interested in is the actual, practical effect of the disputed decision—its consequences for other litigants and in other situations." In other words, the justices care about the ultimate *effect* of the legal policy they set. The justices recognize that the legal rules or precedents established in the Court's majority opinions represent their most important tool for influencing social, political, and economic outcomes. Their behavior on the bench is therefore principally motivated by the distributional consequences of their opinions, and they want these consequences to reflect their preferences.

The evidence of the importance of policy preferences in the decision making of the justices is so convincing that many theoretical approaches start with the assumption that the justices are principally motivated by their preferences over legal policy (e.g., Caldeira, Wright, and Zorn 1999; Cameron, Segal, and Songer 2000; Epstein and Knight 1998; Gely and Spiller 1992; Maltzman, Spriggs, and Wahlbeck 2000). For example, Epstein and Knight (1998, 9–10) state that "judicial specialists generally agree that justices, first and foremost, wish to see their policy preferences etched into law. They are, in the opinion of many, 'single-minded seekers of legal policy.'" Maltzman, Spriggs, and Wahlbeck (2000, 17) refer to this tenet as the "Outcome Postulate" of Supreme Court decision making, which holds that "Justices prefer Court opinions and legal rules that reflect their policy preferences."

We follow this theoretical tradition and make the assumption that the justices want to influence legal policy in a way which leads to outcomes consistent with their preferences. Further assuming that their behavior is goal-oriented, the justices will choose when and how to interpret precedent based on their desire both to create new, efficacious legal policy that reflects their policy preferences and to shift existing legal policy closer to their preferred position. Shortly, we will discuss the specific implications of policy-oriented motivations for the interpretation of precedent.

THE ROLE OF PRECEDENT

The American judicial system is premised in large part on the principle of *stare decisis*, which is the norm requiring that judges follow precedent. As Alexander Hamilton put it in Federalist 78, "[judges] should be bound down by strict rules and precedents, which serve to define and point out their duty in every particular case that comes before them." Precedents are the legal rulings from prior court cases that establish which case facts are relevant (Richards and Kritzer 2002) and create legal consequences or tests that attach to particular sets of factual circumstances (Aldisert 1990; Schauer 1987). The essence of *stare decisis* is that judges should treat like cases alike by applying the legal principles from prior cases to the similar factual circumstances in present cases.

Legal reasoning and *stare decisis* operate as inductive processes. Law develops as judges draw general principles from specific prior cases and determine how to apply those rules to new factual circumstances (see Levi 1949; Wahlbeck 1997). The use of precedent is thus typically depicted as reasoning by example, where the case law set by a precedent is the example and the judge applies it to a present case (Aldisert 1990; Schauer 1987). The core purpose of precedent in this process is to provide judges with information about how to compare and group factual circumstances so that they can be treated similarly. In the process of determining these legal rules, judges decide specific disputes, and, in so doing, affect the meaning and reach of precedents.

Scholars (Epstein and Knight 1998; Friedman et al. 1981; Knight and Epstein 1996) and judges (Powell 1990; Stevens 1983; Wald 1995) commonly aver that one of the most important functions of *stare decisis* is fostering the legitimacy of the judiciary as an institution and the legitimacy of specific court decisions.[1] In fact, some legal historians suggest that the norm of *stare decisis* in American law resulted in part from a crisis in the legitimacy of the federal judiciary in the early to middle part of the 1800s.[2] By avoiding an openly political role and by adopting neutral, principled decision-making criteria, judges enhanced the institutional reputation of the federal judiciary (Friedman 1985, 127–33). Since then, judges have placed great value on the legitimacy of their courts and decisions.

Judges promote legitimacy because they recognize that it encourages acceptance of and compliance with their decisions (Gibson 1989; Mondak 1990, 1994; Tyler and Mitchell 1994). In our view of Supreme Court decision making, the justices value legitimacy for instrumental reasons, namely, as a means to the end of producing efficacious policy (see Epstein and Knight 1998). As discussed more fully below, court decisions are not self-executing and thus third parties must implement them before they have any real effects. Since legitimacy encourages compliance, it enhances the power of courts and facilitates their ability to cause legal and political change. Landes and Posner (1976, 273) make this point when stating: "No matter how willful a judge is, he is likely to follow precedent to some extent, for if he did not the practice of decision according to prece-

---

[1] The norm of precedent reportedly serves a variety of other goals, including judicial efficiency (Landes and Posner 1976; Shapiro 1965), stability and predictability in the law (Stevens 1983), justice and fairness (see Douglas [1949] 1979; Maltz 1988; Schauer 1987; Shapiro 1972), legal clarity (Bueno de Mesquita and Stephenson 2002), and future judicial compliance (Rasmusen 1994).

[2] Prior to the mid-1800s, most legal historians indicate that in the United States there was no "firm doctrine of *stare decisis*" (Kempin 1959, 50), and "the whole theory and practice of precedent was in a highly fluctuating condition" (Allen 1964, 209).

dent (*stare decisis*, the lawyers call it) would be undermined and the precedential significance of his own decisions thereby reduced." Justice Stevens (1983, 2) reiterates this point by noting that *stare decisis* "obviously enhances the institutional strength of the judiciary."

The significance of institutional and decisional legitimacy follows from two well-known characteristics of the judiciary. While these features apply to all courts, we will discuss them in the context relevant for our purposes—the U.S. Supreme Court. First, unlike elected officials or bureaucrats, the justices are expected to provide neutral, legal justifications for their decisions (Friedman et al. 1981; Maltz 1988). One important element of this expectation is that the justices show respect for the Court's prior decisions (Powell 1990). A recent national survey, for instance, demonstrates that the American public expects the Court to decide based on legal factors (Scheb and Lyons 2001). Nearly eighty-five percent of respondents to this survey indicated that precedent should have some or a large impact on the justices' decisions. By contrast, over seventy-three percent of respondents thought that whether judges were Democrats or Republicans should have no influence on their decisions. As these data indicate, Americans overwhelmingly believe in the idea that judges should make decisions based on neutral, legal criteria.

Second, the Court lacks significant implementation powers and thus relies on its external reputation to encourage implementation of and compliance with its decisions. Alexander Hamilton pointed this idea out in Federalist 78: "The judiciary on the contrary has no influence over either the sword or the purse, no direction either of the strength or of the wealth of the society, and can take no active resolution whatever. It may truly be said to have neither Force nor Will, but merely judgment; and must ultimately depend upon the aid of the executive arm for the efficacy of its judgments." The basic idea is that the Court must rely on third parties to implement its policies, and a central way to promote compliance is through fostering institutional and decisional legitimacy (see Knight and Epstein 1996). If the Court, or a particular majority opinion, is perceived as somewhat illegitimate, then the prospects for compliance may decrease. The power of the Court, that is, rests on its "prestige to persuade" (Ginsburg 2004, 199).

We emphasize that the legitimizing effect of precedent stems from its perception as a neutral, legal decision criterion. Survey data, for example, indicate that the principal reason individuals see the Court as a legitimate institution is because they perceive it as being procedurally fair (Tyler and Mitchell 1994). Tyler and Mitchell (1994, 786) conclude that: "Justices who are viewed as honest, impartial, and deliberative, basing their decisions on case-relevant information, rather than as driven by political pressures and personal opinion, are performing legitimately in the eyes of the public." The justices agree with the idea that their capacity to rule hinges on legitimacy (see *Bush v. Vera* 1996; *Planned Parenthood v. Casey* 1992; *Vasquez v. Hillery* 1986; Powell 1990; Stevens 1983). As the Court notes in *Vasquez v. Hillery* (1986): "That doctrine [*stare decisis*] permits society to presume that bedrock principles are founded in the law rather than in the proclivities of individuals, and thereby contributes to the integrity of our constitutional system of government, both in appearance and in fact" (474 U.S. 254, 265–66).

This discussion leads to the following point; one of the principal reasons that courts write opinions and utilize precedent is to legitimize their policy choices through the invocation of neutral decision-making criteria.[3] The justices recognize the social expectation that they justify their policies, and they understand that this belief can affect whether and to what extent decision makers accept and comply with Court decisions (Powell 1990; Stevens 1983). Judge Patricia Wald (1995, 1372) recognizes this point when noting that judges publish opinions to promote their "credibility." Judge Wald (1995, 1372) writes, "One of the few ways we [judges] have to justify our power to decide matters important to our fellow citizens is to explain why we decide as we do." The justices therefore utilize precedent and link current decisions to past rules of law (Johnson 1986; Phelps and Gates 1991; Walsh 1997). In sum, the use of and adherence to precedent can produce external legitimacy and thereby enhance the Court's ability to write opinions that have influence.

Given the justices' need to legitimize their policies, precedent can limit their flexibility or discretion. It does so by constraining the alternatives available to the justices to those which are legally defensible (van Hees and Steunenberg 2000). By this, we mean legal holdings and reasoning that the justices can credibly argue are founded on a legally relevant basis. In a given case, precedent may eliminate particular alternatives from consideration. Lawyers recognize this facet of judicial decision making and develop arguments in their briefs based on precedent in an effort to narrow the range of alternatives available to a court (Shapiro 1965, 148). Supreme Court justices also recognize this feature of the judiciary, as noted in *Planned Parenthood v. Casey* (1992): "Thus, the Court's legitimacy depends on making legally principled decisions under circum-

---

[3] Adherence to the norm of *stare decisis* is not the only means by which courts can increase the degree to which their decisions are perceived as legitimate. Epstein, Segal, and Johnson (1996), for instance, argue that Supreme Court justices are reluctant to address issues not raised by the litigants because such behavior would reduce the legitimacy of their decisions. Attempts at consensual decision making have also been motivated by the desire to maximize legitimacy (Epstein, Segal, and Spaeth 2001).

stances in which their principled character is sufficiently plausible to be accepted by the Nation" (505 U.S. 833, 865).

In any given case, there may be a number of legally defensible positions, and thus our conception of precedent does not suggest that it leads ineluctably to particular outcomes. Scholars (see Carter 1988; Dworkin 1978; Murphy, Fleming, and Barber 1995, 30–33; Shapiro 1965) and jurists (Cardozo [1921] 1964; Wald 1995) recognize that judges continue to have discretion even in the face of the norm of *stare decisis*. For example, Supreme Court justices rarely decide two cases on the merits with precisely the same facts, and in many cases there may be conflicting precedent on an issue. Thus, there is often decisional leeway in determining whether a precedent governs a case (see Carter 1988; Schauer 1987).

Two quotes from jurists eloquently make the point that judicial discretion exists alongside *stare decisis*. Benjamin Cardozo (1964, 103) wrote: "We [judges] must keep within those interstitial limits which precedent and custom . . . have set to judge-made innovations. But within the limits thus set, within the range over which choice moves, the final principle of selection for judges, as for legislators, is one of fitness to an end." Judge Wald (1995, 1399) echoes this position: "In most cases there are prior circuit cases or Supreme Court cases whose rulings and rhetoric are relevant, but it is still a judgment call for the court whether they require a particular outcome in the immediate case."

In sum, we contend that *stare decisis* plays a key role in Court decision making due to the justices' need to legitimize their policy choices. The justices recognize that the legitimacy of a decision is a necessary condition for it to produce the distributional effects they desire. In deciding current disputes, the justices therefore pay attention to precedent and incorporate it into their opinions. In so doing, they can provide neutral, legal justifications for their decisions and thereby enhance their legitimacy. This norm, however, operates in such a way that justices continue to have significant discretion. While we do not suggest that precedent is necessarily binding or argue, for example, that precedent will inevitably change a justice's vote on the merits (see Spaeth and Segal 1999), we do contend that this norm creates incentives for the justices to respond to precedent in predictable ways.

The norm of *stare decisis* also grants the Court power because it is a means of influencing the choices of other political and nonpolitical decision makers. Lower court judges, in particular, are expected to follow the precedents established by the Supreme Court, and thus this norm provides the Court with an opportunity to influence broadly policy outcomes. In other words, without the norm of *stare decisis*, precedent would be considerably less meaningful and the Court's ability to act as an important policy maker would be highly diminished. We now turn to a discussion of an important aspect of *stare decisis*—the legal vitality of a precedent.

Precedent Vitality

Precedents vary in their legal vitality, or the extent to which they maintain legal authority (see Aldisert 1990; Peczenik 1997). Some precedents are more legally authoritative than others and thus have an enhanced ability to justify and legitimize the justices' policy choices. We refer to this element of *stare decisis* as "precedent vitality." The norm of *stare decisis* implies that, for legitimacy reasons, the justices are more likely to rely on those precedents possessing greater legal weight. We therefore argue that the justices recognize variation in the vitality of precedent and respond accordingly.

Although the specific term "vitality" is not always used, the concept of precedent vitality is commonly discussed. It is referred to by justices in their opinions,[4] pointed to by lawyers in their legal briefs,[5] debated in law review articles (e.g., Bhala 1999; Stern 1989), and discussed by judges in their off-the-bench writings (e.g., Aldisert 1990; Schaefer 2004; Wald 1995). These sources generally agree that, in the words of Judge Aldisert (1990, 631), not all precedents "have the same bite." They also typically suggest that precedent vitality has implications for the interpretation of precedent and legal change (Johnson 1987; Peczenik 1997). But, this idea has yet to be firmly conceptualized and incorporated into systematic analyses of court usage of precedent.

The literature discusses a variety of possible factors that could be linked with precedent vitality, most notably characteristics of the precedent, such as the size of the decision coalition supporting the precedent (Brenner and Spaeth 1995, 46; Johnson 1987), the presence of separate opinions (e.g., Aldisert 1990, 632; Danelski 1986; Johnson 1987; Pacelle and Baum 1992; Peczenik 1997), and the age of the precedent (Kosma 1998; Landes and Posner 1976). With the exception of precedent age, these factors are static in nature and do not fluctuate over the life of a precedent. As a result, they are not linked to the ebb and flow of the vitality of a precedent over time. Our argument centers on the notion that the vitality of a precedent can change over time, and thus our theoretical

[4] For some recent examples, see *Harris v. United States* (2002), *Circuit City Stores v. Adams* (2001), *United States v. Morrison* (2000), and Justice O'Connor's dissent in *Tuan Anh Nguyen v. I.N.S.* (2001).

[5] For example, see the amicus briefs filed by the State of New Jersey in *Grutter v. Bollinger* (2003), by a number of law professors in *Green Tree Financial Corp. v. Bazzle* (2003), and by Henry Waxman et al. in *American Insurance Association v. Garamendi* (2003).

framework does not place emphasis on these factors. Nonetheless, the empirical models presented in subsequent chapters do control for them as possible influences on the interpretation of precedent.

There are two reasons why our conceptualization of precedent vitality does not hinge on precedent age. First, as political scientists we are interested in studying variables that reveal the politics of judging. We therefore wish to focus on an aspect of precedent vitality that can be directly influenced by the behavior of judges. The age of a precedent, however, is outside the control of a judge and thus is not of central theoretical interest to us. Second, it is not immediately clear what effect age will have on the vitality of a precedent. An argument could be made that older precedents might be more institutionalized and thus possess greater vitality (see Benesh and Reddick 2002; Brenner and Spaeth 1995, 11).[6] Alternatively, it could be argued that older precedents are more removed from contemporary legal questions and thus are less relevant (see Landes and Posner 1976). Indeed, it is likely that some precedents become more vital over time as they become an increasingly solid foundation for subsequent decisions and precedents, while others become less vital as they are chipped away. We contend that it is not the age of the precedent that determines its vitality. It is the treatment that the precedent receives by the Court over time that will influence its vitality.[7]

We therefore conceptualize the vitality of a precedent as deriving from the Supreme Court's interpretation of it in other cases. This focus follows from our contention that the meaning of a precedent is not fixed but can fluctuate over time as the Court decides whether and how to apply it to new factual settings. As the Court interprets a precedent and decides, for example, to extend it in new circumstances or limit it to its facts, the reach and scope of the precedent changes. This process is what Levi (1949) and Wahlbeck (1997) have in mind when they argue that legal development occurs as judges confront novel factual circumstances and determine whether to include or exclude them from the relevant legal rule. Thus, theoretically speaking, the meaning and clout of a precedent hangs centrally on how the Court treats it in subsequent cases.

This variation in the authority of precedent has important implications for the Court's ability to legitimize its policies. If the Court has positively

---

[6] Bueno de Mesquita and Stephenson (2002) also suggest that precedent age, to the extent that it reflects the number of progeny cases following the precedent-setting case, increases the clarity or informational content of the precedent. One problem with this idea is that it does not recognize that the positive or negative treatment of precedent has differential effects on a precedent's vitality and, as we show below, therefore alters the benefits the justices receive from subsequently interpreting it.

[7] We will, though, be careful to control for any age-related effects when estimating our statistical models.

interpreted a precedent, it takes on greater authority, is more institutionalized, and hence has greater legal weight (see Aldisert 1990, 632; Ulmer 1959). The positive interpretation of a precedent occurs when a Court opinion explicitly states that it is controlling authority for the dispute. This action helps to bolster the authority of the precedent and possibly expand its scope. As a result, precedents that have been positively interpreted by the Court in the past provide good vehicles for justifying current Court outcomes. Landes and Posner (1976, 250) note that: "Where, however, the rule has been, as it were, solidified in a long line of decisions, the authority of the rule is enhanced." The Court can therefore maximize the legitimacy of an opinion by relying on precedent that has received prior positive Court treatment.

If, by contrast, the Court has negatively interpreted a precedent, then that precedent's legal authority is diminished (Douglas [1949] 1979; Stern 1989; Wald 1995). By interpreting a precedent negatively, the Court, at a minimum, can distinguish a case and indicate that it does not apply to a new factual circumstance. At the extreme, the Court can overrule a case, and declare that it is no longer controlling law (see Murphy and Pritchett 1979, 491–95). This form of legal treatment thus declares some level of disagreement with the precedent and may undercut its applicability and authority for other legal disputes. As Judge Patricia Wald (1995, 1399) notes, "Over time, precedent . . . widely criticized loses its vitality." Negative interpretation therefore serves to narrow the reach of a precedent and weaken its vitality. Prior negative interpretation also makes it easier or less costly, in terms of legitimacy, for the Court to treat it negatively in the future.

Let us now connect this discussion of precedent vitality more directly with the legitimizing function of *stare decisis*. Our contention is that a Court decision is more likely to be perceived as legitimate, by those who are aware of it (namely, those who are tasked with interpreting or implementing it), if the justices justify it with legally vital precedents. By justifying a decision with more legally authoritative precedents, the justices emphasize its principled basis. As was pointed out above, one significant component of an individual's perception of the legitimacy of a decision is whether it was made on a principled, neutral basis. If decision makers implementing a decision, for example, perceive it as less legitimate, then they will be less likely to comply with it (Gibson 1989; Tyler 1984, 1990; Tyler and Mitchell 1994; Tyler and Rasinksi 1991).

It is important for us to clarify the assumptions underlying the connection between legal vitality and legitimacy. First, we assume that the legal vitality of cited precedents affects the legitimacy of individual decisions. We do not assume that the Court's use of precedent in any one opinion will affect the Court's overall institutional legitimacy. Since most people will not be familiar with the manner in which the Court uses precedent in any given opinion, it is unlikely that one decision will greatly affect the Court's overall legitimacy.[8] For individuals who are aware of a particular decision, however, we suggest that their perception of its legitimacy is likely to differ based on the Court's use of precedent in it.

Second, our argument does not require that the mass public be cognizant of whether the justices rely on legally vital precedents in their decisions. Instead, we suggest that the most relevant decision makers in this regard are those who must interpret or implement an opinion, as well as potential future litigants. They will be familiar with the basis of the Court's decision, including the manner in which the justices use precedent.[9] Consider, for instance, the most relevant decision maker in this regard, lower court judges. When interpreting a decision, they will obviously be familiar with the manner in which the Court incorporated precedent into it. Thus, we suggest that it is only necessary for particular sets of individuals, most notably those who will interpret and implement the decision (see Canon and Johnson 1999), to be aware of the Court's use of precedent in a decision.

Finally, even if the vitality of cited precedents has little actual effect on the legitimacy of the citing decision, as long as the justices believe that this connection exists, then they will take precedent vitality into consideration. In Court opinions[10] and off-the-bench comments (Ginsburg 2004; Powell 1990; Wald 1995) justices and judges go to great lengths to perpetuate the idea that the Court is a principled decision maker. They do so out of a recognition that the Court's power rests on its legitimacy. The day after the Court decided *Bush v. Gore* (2000), for example, Justice Thomas told a group of high school students that politics played no role at the Court: "I have yet to hear any discussion, in nine years, of partisan politics among the justices. I plead with you that, whatever you do, try to apply the rules of the political world to this institution; they do not apply" (qtd. in Greenhouse 2000, A1). This idea is even more apparent in *Planned Parenthood v. Casey* (1992), where the Court argued that

---

[8] On rare occasion, however, such an effect may occur. Nicholson and Howard (2002), for example, show that, when framed in certain ways, the American public's confidence in the justices declined after *Bush v. Gore*. Generally speaking, scholars argue that the Court's behavior can influence its overall institutional standing (Caldeira 1986; Grosskopf and Mondak 1998; Mondak and Smithey 1997), although others disagree (Gibson and Caldeira 1992).

[9] These decision makers can easily learn about the vitality of a precedent by using *Shepard's Citations*, which is the standard source used by judges and lawyers for learning about the current legal authority of a case.

[10] See *Bush v. Vera* (1996); *Planned Parenthood v. Casey* (1992); *Vasquez v. Hillery* (1986).

its legitimacy would be undermined by overruling *Roe*: "A decision to overrule *Roe*'s essential holding . . . [would cause] both profound and unnecessary damage to the Court's legitimacy" (505 U.S. 833, 869).

To summarize, the justices recognize the need to legitimize their policy choices by basing them on precedent. But, not all precedents are equally capable of justifying a Court decision. The Court's ability to justify, and thus legitimize, current policies depends in part on the vitality of the precedents relied on in a decision. The incorporation and treatment of cases with greater legal authority better serves to legitimize the Court's current decisions in the eyes of those who have an interest in them, most notably those interpreting or implementing them. Importantly, the vitality of a precedent can change over time as the Court positively or negatively interprets it. Vitality, thus, is a dynamic property of a precedent that fluctuates over time based on the Court's treatment of it in other cases. The justices therefore have incentives, deriving from the norm of *stare decisis*, to consider the legal vitality of a precedent when choosing whether and how to interpret it.

While much of the discussion of precedent vitality and the legitimacy of Court decisions has been couched in terms of the legitimacy *benefits* associated with positively incorporating a vital precedent, it is important to note the flip side to this argument. The Court will also be concerned with the potential legitimacy *costs* incurred by treating precedents in a negative fashion. Just as there are greater legitimacy benefits to following a particularly vital precedent, there are greater legitimacy costs to overruling or otherwise undermining a precedent that is highly vital.

WHY THE COURT INTERPRETS PRECEDENT

Now that we have generally introduced the basic elements that will shape our argument, we can begin to develop a specific theoretical answer to the question of when and why the Court will positively or negatively interpret a precedent. We contend that there are two motivations driving the interpretation of precedent, both of which bear on the justices' ultimate desire to influence distributional outcomes in a manner consistent with their personal policy preferences. The first motivation is to shape existing precedents so that they better reflect the preferences of the justices. This factor is relevant because a necessary, but not sufficient, condition for favorable policy outcomes is that Court precedent is consistent with the justices' preferences.

The second motivation behind the interpretation of precedent is to justify and promote the legitimacy of new policy choices contained in the Court's contemporary majority opinions. Since the Court cannot truly implement its decisions or legal policies, the justices must rely on the perceived legitimacy of a decision to enhance the likelihood that other decision makers will implement or comply with it.

Thus, the utility associated with the interpretation of a precedent is a combination of the benefits associated with altering the current status of the precedent and legitimizing the new legal policy established by the Court.[11] We first turn to a discussion of the utility of interpreting a precedent positively and afterwards address the utility of negative interpretation.

The Positive Interpretation of Precedent

When will the Supreme Court choose to interpret a precedent in a positive manner? If the benefit or utility of interpreting a precedent depends upon the benefits resulting from potential effects on the scope and content of extant legal policy and the legitimacy of new legal policy, then the utility of the positive interpretation of a precedent simply can be represented as:

$$u(positive\ interpretation) = influence\ over\ extant\ policy$$
$$+ legitimization\ of\ new\ policy$$

We address these two elements of the utility of positive interpretation in turn.

INFLUENCE OVER EXTANT POLICY

The Court can strengthen a precedent by interpreting it in a positive manner. Through this type of interpretation, the justices can broaden the precedent's legal basis, make it applicable to a wider set of factual scenarios, or simply reaffirm its continuing authority. The utility the justices receive from positively interpreting a precedent derives in part from the degree to which they agree with the precedent in question. The more in-line the precedent is with the sitting justices' policy preferences, the greater the benefit (in terms of influence over extant policy) they receive from interpreting it positively. By contrast, the more ideologically distant the justices are from a precedent, the smaller the benefit of interpreting the precedent positively.

This element of the utility associated with positive interpretation will also depend on the current vitality of the precedent in question. If the

---

[11] We need to be clear that our theoretical framework is not a formal expected utility model. Rather, we use the mathematical expressions below as a way to lay bare the assumptions and principles guiding our analysis and to delineate clearly the predictions deriving from the model.

justices are ideologically close to a precedent and the precedent has been weakened in the past, then there is an even greater policy incentive to bolster the vitality of this precedent by treating it positively. The positive interpretation of the precedent may increase its applicability in lower courts and otherwise revive the importance of an ideologically favored precedent. There is less of a policy incentive, relatively speaking, for the justices to positively treat an ideologically proximate precedent if the precedent is already quite vital. The ultimate effect of positive interpretation on the legal reach of a precedent is greater when the favored precedent is currently weak.

If a precedent is ideologically incongruent with the Court, then the vitality of the precedent should exert the opposite effect. While the Court always derives less utility from positively interpreting an ideologically distant precedent, the Court has an even smaller incentive to do so if the precedent is less vital. A positive interpretation of a less vital case can strengthen it and thereby lead other decision makers to rely upon it, when they had not been doing so in the past. As a result, a positive interpretation of an ideologically distant precedent that is less vital can make the justices worse off (in a policy sense) than the positive interpretation of such a precedent that is already quite vital. The Court will therefore most prefer to bolster weak precedents that are ideologically congruent with the Court and will least prefer to strengthen weak precedents that are incongruent with the Court.

It is important for us to point out that we are not suggesting that the Court will ever become more likely to positively interpret precedents as ideological distance increases. We are simply claiming that the small benefit or cost associated with positively interpreting an ideologically distant precedent will diminish even further if the precedent is not vital, for the same reason that the Court prefers to positively interpret ideologically close precedents that are less vital.

Thus, the vitality of a precedent conditions the effect that ideological distance exerts on this element of the utility of positive interpretation. Precedent vitality increases the value of positively interpreting an ideologically distant precedent, relatively speaking, and decreases the value of positively treating an ideologically close precedent. In this sense, precedent vitality attenuates the effect of ideological distance in that ideological distance exerts a greater effect on the utility of treating a low-vitality precedent positively than a high-vitality precedent. We can represent this argument with the following weighted combination:

$$influence \ over \ extant \ policy = -b_1(ID) + b_2(ID \times V) - b_3(V),$$

where ID is the ideological distance between the Court and a precedent and V represents the vitality of the precedent. The positive sign for b_2, in conjunction with the negative sign for b_3, captures our argument that when the Court prefers a precedent it will derive less utility from positively interpreting a precedent that already has a good deal of vitality.[12] Conversely, when comparing ideologically distant precedents, the Court will prefer (in relative terms) to positively treat a precedent that is more vital. Put differently, as ideological distance increases, the effect of vitality will shift from positive to negative, and hence we expect a positive weight or coefficient for the interaction term and a negative coefficient for V.

Our argument here also requires two constraints to be placed on this function:

$$-b_1 + b_2(V_{max}) \leq 0, \text{ where } V_{max} \text{ represents the}$$
$$\text{maximum possible value of } V; \tag{c_1}$$

and

$$b_2(ID) - b_3 < 0 \text{ for the lower range of } ID \text{ and}$$
$$b_2(ID) - b_3 > 0 \text{ for the upper range of } ID. \tag{c_2}$$

The first constraint ensures that the ideological distance between the sitting justices and a precedent (ID) always exerts a negative effect on the utility of treating a precedent positively.[13] This constraint captures the argument that the Court, for policy-based reasons, will never be more likely to interpret a precedent positively as it becomes ideologically further removed from a precedent, regardless of the degree to which the precedent is legally vital. The second constraint captures our argument that the effect of precedent vitality (V) will change direction as ideological distance increases.[14]

LEGITIMIZATION OF NEW POLICY

The second consideration affecting the utility of interpreting a precedent positively is the extent to which the positive interpretation of a precedent increases the legitimacy of the new policy set in a Court decision. By increasing the perceived legitimacy of a decision, the Court improves the prospect that the decision will be implemented, enforced, and thus efficacious. As emphasized earlier in the chapter, we are not arguing that the vitality of the precedents utilized in a Court opinion will have any effect on the extent to which the mass public perceives the Court to be legitimate. We simply contend that among the actors who are aware of the

---

[12] When the Court completely agrees with the policy content of a precedent, ideological distance equals zero, the interaction term thus equals zero, and the total effect of precedent vitality will be $-b_3$.

[13] $-b_1 + b_2(V)$ captures the complete (conditional) effect of ideological distance.

[14] $b_2(ID) - b_3$ captures the complete (conditional) effect of precedent vitality.

Court's decision, most notably those individuals who implement and interpret the decision (such as lower court judges) as well as potential future litigants, the extent to which the new legal policy set by the Court is viewed as legitimate will depend, in part, on how the Court has justified the policy. The norm of *stare decisis* indicates that courts should rely on precedent when deciding cases, and this norm, we argue, implicitly requires courts to place greater weight on the more authoritative or vital precedents.

In the context of our model, this legitimization effect will be determined by the vitality of the precedent. If, for example, a precedent has been treated positively in the past and has not been treated negatively (i.e., the precedent has a high degree of vitality), then it takes on greater authority, is more institutionalized, and hence has greater legal weight (see Aldisert 1990; Landes and Posner 1976; Ulmer 1959). As a result, vital precedents provide good vehicles for justifying current Court outcomes, and the justices can increase the perceived legitimacy of an opinion by relying on such precedents.

If the Court has negatively interpreted a precedent in the past, then that case's legal authority is diminished. The Court's reliance on such a precedent is therefore less likely to contribute to the legitimacy of a new policy. The ideological distance between the Court and the precedent will not play a role in this aspect of the utility function, since the extent to which a precedent will legitimize a decision will be independent of policy considerations. We can represent this element of the Court's utility for positively interpreting a precedent as:

legitimization of new policy $= b_4(V)$.

THE UTILITY OF POSITIVE INTERPRETATION

To establish the utility the Court receives from interpreting precedent positively, we combine *influence over extant policy* and *legitimization of new policy* to yield the following:

$$u(positive\ interpretation) = -b_1(ID) + b_2(ID \times V) + (b_4 - b_3)(V).$$

The constraints from *influence over extant policy* remain in place:

$$-b_1 + b_2(V_{max}) \leq 0; \tag{c_1}$$

and

$$b_2(ID) - b_3 < 0 \text{ for the lower range of } ID \text{ and}$$
$$b_2(ID) - b_3 > 0 \text{ for the upper range of } ID. \tag{c_2}$$

Assuming that the probability of the Court treating a precedent positively will be determined by the benefits or utility associated with this choice, this function yields the following propositions. First, the ideological distance between the Court and a precedent will have a negative effect on the probability of the Court treating the precedent positively, since increases in ideological distance decrease the utility associated with this type of interpretation.

> *Proposition 2.1: The smaller the ideological distance between a precedent and the Court, the more likely the Court is to positively interpret it (reflected by $-b_1$ and c_1).*

The second general proposition is that the vitality of a precedent will condition the effect of ideological distance on the probability of the Court treating the precedent positively. Ideological distance exerts a greater negative effect on the likelihood of treating a low-vitality precedent positively than on the likelihood of treating a high-vitality precedent in such a manner.

> *Proposition 2.2: As precedent vitality increases, the negative effect of ideological distance on the probability of positive treatment will be attenuated (reflected by b_2 and c_1).*

Our theory is agnostic regarding the relative magnitudes of the effect of precedent vitality as seen in the justices' desire to influence existing Court policy (b_3) and the role of precedent vitality in their need to legitimize new policy choices (b_4). As a result, we cannot make a prediction for the direct effect of precedent vitality on the probability of the Court interpreting a precedent positively. When there is no ideological distance between the Court and a precedent (i.e., the precedent is perfectly compatible with Court preferences), then $ID \times V$ is zero and the effect of precedent vitality is captured solely by $b_4 - b_3$. Not having an ex ante expectation regarding the relative size of these two weights, we cannot predict the influence of vitality for precedents that are ideologically compatible with the Court. If b_4 is larger than b_3, then vitality will exert a positive effect when a precedent is perfectly compatible with the Court. If b_3 is larger than b_4, then vitality will exert a negative effect when a precedent is perfectly compatible with the Court. Therefore, while we can predict the manner in which vitality conditions the effect of ideological distance, we cannot predict shifts in the intercept that result from different values of precedent vitality. In our various empirical analyses, however, we will be able to generate estimates of ($b_4 - b_3$) and thus determine which influence is larger.

We can identify a third proposition, though, that involves the effect of precedent vitality on the likelihood of the Court treating a precedent positively. Based on the constraint that $b_2(ID) - b_3$ is greater than zero for the upper range of ID, it follows that when ideological distance is great, precedent vitality will have a positive effect on the probability of positive treatment. If $b_2(ID) - b_3$ is positive for the upper range of ideological distance and b_4 is always positive, then the full effect of vitality, $b_2(ID) - b_3 + b_4$, must also be positive for the upper range of ideological distance. This logic indicates that while we cannot predict the direct effect of precedent vitality on the likelihood of the precedent being positively interpreted when ideological distance is low, we can predict that the effect will be positive when ideological distance is high.

> *Proposition 2.3: For precedents that are ideologically distant from the Court, increases in precedent vitality will increase the probability of positive interpretation (based on b_4 and c_1).*

To further illustrate these points and provide a better feel for our propositions more generally, figure 2.1 presents three possible scenarios consistent with our model. The difference across the three scenarios involves the relative magnitudes of b_3 and b_4, about which, as discussed above, we have no theoretical prediction. In the first scenario b_3 is greater in magnitude than b_4, while in the second and third scenarios b_3 is equal to b_4 and b_3 is smaller than b_4, respectively. For all scenarios, the utility, and thus probability, of treating a precedent positively decreases as ideological distance increases (Proposition 1), and this decrease is steepest for low vitality precedents (Proposition 2). Ideologically distant precedents are also more likely to be treated positively if they have a high degree of vitality. Put differently, in all three scenarios vitality increases the likelihood of positive interpretation for precedents that are ideologically distant from the Court (Proposition 3). For all three scenarios, when ideological distance is high the high vitality precedent is more likely to be positively interpreted than the low vitality precedent.

The differences in the relative magnitude of weights b_3 and b_4 across these three scenarios do affect the intercept of the lines, however. Depending on the relative magnitude of these weights, precedent vitality can either increase or decrease the probability of positively interpreting a precedent that is ideologically compatible with the Court. If the justices' desire to influence the state of existing policy dominates ($b_3 > b_4$), then scenario 1 results and precedent vitality will increase the utility of positively interpreting ideologically distant precedents and decrease the utility for ideologically close precedents. If the justices' desire to maximize the legitimacy of the new precedent being created dominates ($b_3 < b_4$), then the Court will always prefer to positively treat highly vital precedents as opposed to less-vital precedents (scenario 3). The second scenario, in which precedent vitality always exerts a positive effect except for when ideological distance is at its minimum, will occur when these

Scenario 1:

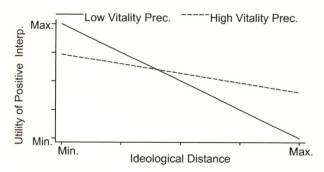

Scenario 2:

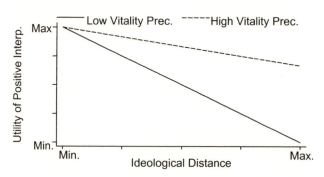

Scenario 3:

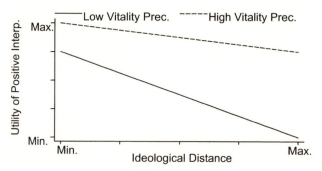

Figure 2.1. Scenarios consistent with our theoretical model of the positive interpretation of precedent

two concerns are equally important. In subsequent chapters, we will be able to ascertain empirically which of these scenarios most closely reflects reality. In so doing, we can speak directly to whether the role of vitality in the justices' desire to move existing policy into conformance with their policy preferences or the effect of vitality on the legitimization of new policy choices has a stronger pull.

The Negative Interpretation of Precedent

When will the Court interpret a precedent in a negative manner (e.g., limit or distinguish the precedent)? If, as above, the utility of interpreting a precedent depends upon the benefits associated with the potential influence on extant policy and the legitimacy of new policy, then the utility of a negative interpretation of a precedent can also be represented as:

$$u(negative\ interpretation) = influence\ over\ extant\ policy$$
$$+ legitimization\ of\ new\ policy.$$

We now turn to these separate elements.

INFLUENCE OVER EXTANT POLICY

In pursuing their policy goals, the justices wish to produce legal policies that influence outcomes in ways consistent with their policy preferences. One way they can do so is by negatively interpreting a precedent and thus weakening its legal authority. The justices will derive greater benefit from negatively interpreting precedents that are ideologically distant from them. By contrast, the closer a precedent is ideologically to the sitting justices, the less benefit they receive from interpreting it negatively.

The effect of ideological distance on the benefit associated with negatively altering the status of a precedent also depends on the current legal vitality of the precedent in question. When considering ideologically distant precedents, the justices will derive more benefit from reducing the applicability of a vital precedent, as opposed to negatively treating a precedent that has already been significantly weakened. Precedents that already have a low degree of vitality are less likely to be exerting much influence over lower courts or other relevant decision makers. As a result, there is less incentive to negatively interpret weakened precedents with which the justices disagree, as opposed to vital precedents that continue to influence policy outcomes.

When considering a precedent preferred by the justices, greater precedent vitality will further diminish the already small value associated with treating this precedent negatively. The justices have more to lose when negatively interpreting vital (rather than nonvital) precedents with which they agree on policy grounds. The vital precedents are presumably influencing distributional consequences, while the nonvital precedents are having less of an effect. While the justices are always loath to negatively treat precedents that comport with their policy goals, they are even more reluctant to do so when that precedent is legally authoritative.

Thus, the vitality of a precedent will condition the effect of ideological distance on the benefit associated with influencing the state of existing precedent. We can represent this in the following manner:

$$influence\ over\ extant\ policy = b_5(ID) + b_6(ID \times V) - b_7(V),$$

where

$b_6(ID) - b_7 < 0$ for the lower range of ID, and

$b_6(ID) - b_7 > 0$ for the upper range of ID.[15]

(c_3)

This function indicates, first, that the justices are more likely to negatively treat precedents which are further removed from their policy goals. It also predicts that when ideological distance is low, the benefit of treating a precedent negatively will decrease as the vitality of the precedent increases. As the ideological distance between the justices and a precedent increases, however, the effect of vitality will change in direction (which is guaranteed by the constraints) and vitality will exert a positive effect on the probability of the Court treating the precedent in a negative fashion.[16] In other words, the justices have more to gain, as far as influencing extant policy is concerned, from negatively interpreting a vital (rather than a nonvital) precedent with which they disagree. Conversely, vitality will exert a negative effect for precedents that are compatible with the Court's preferences. Put yet another way, increases in precedent vitality amplify the effect of ideological distance on the benefit associated with treating a precedent negatively.

LEGITIMIZATION OF NEW POLICY

As a result of the norm of *stare decisis*, the Court can incur legitimacy costs by negatively interpreting a vital or institutionalized precedent. If instead of following a highly institutionalized, bedrock precedent (i.e., a highly vital precedent) the Court chooses to treat the precedent in a negative manner, then the new policy set by the Court may be perceived as being less legitimate. In other words, just as there are greater legitimacy benefits to following a particularly vital precedent, there are potentially

---

[15] We do not need an equivalent of the first constraint in the positive interpretation model (c_1) here because the positive direction of b_5 and b_6 guarantees that ideological distance will always have a positive effect on the utility of interpreting a precedent negatively.

[16] This effect will occur when $b_2(ID)$ is greater than the absolute value of $-b_3$.

greater legitimacy costs to overruling or otherwise undermining a precedent that is highly vital. There will be less of a legitimacy cost, on the other hand, when the Court negatively interprets a precedent that is not particularly institutionalized or authoritative.

The vitality of a precedent, therefore, determines the extent to which the justices bear a legitimacy cost when negatively interpreting the precedent. The more vital a precedent is, the greater the cost that results from treating the precedent negatively. The ideological distance between the justices and the precedent has no effect on the costliness, in terms of legitimacy, resulting from negative treatment. This argument can be represented as:

$$legitimization\ of\ new\ policy = -b_8(V).$$

THE UTILITY OF NEGATIVE INTERPRETATION

By combining the above two components of the utility associated with negatively treating a precedent, we obtain the following:

$$u(negative\ interpretation) = b_5(ID) + b_6(ID \times V) - (b_7 + b_8)(V),$$

where

$b_6(ID) - b_7 < 0$ for the lower range of ID, and

$b_6(ID) - b_7 > 0$ for the upper range of ID. $\hspace{1cm}$ (c$_1$)

If the likelihood of the Court treating a precedent negatively is determined by the utility associated with this type of interpretation, then this function contains the following general propositions.

> *Proposition 2.4: The greater the ideological distance between the Court and a precedent, the greater the likelihood that the Court will negatively interpret the precedent (based on b_5 and b_6).*

> *Proposition 2.5: The positive effect of ideological distance on the probability of negative interpretation will increase in magnitude as a precedent becomes more vital (based on b_6).*

> *Proposition 2.6: For precedents favored by the Court, increases in precedent vitality will lower the probability of negative interpretation (based on $-(b_7 + b_8)$ and constraint 3).[17]*

[17] If $b_6(ID) - b_7 < 0$ for the lower range of ID, then $b_6(ID) - b_7 - b_8$ must also be less than zero for the lower range of ID.

Scenario 1:

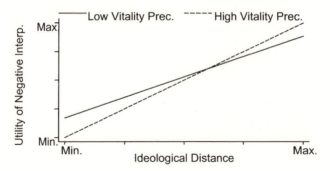

Scenario 2:

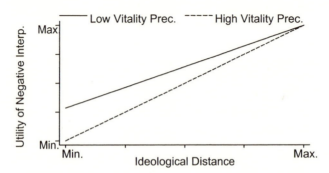

Scenario 3:

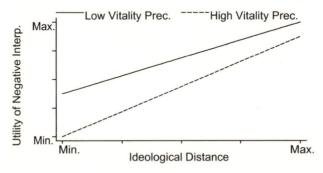

Figure 2.2. Scenarios consistent with our theoretical model of the negative interpretation of precedent

Our theory does not lead to a prediction for the effect of vitality when ideological distance is high because while $b_6(ID) - b_7 > 0$ for the upper range of *Ideological Distance* (ID), $b_6(ID) - b_7 - b_8$ could be greater or less than zero for the higher values of *ID*. We therefore do not predict the effect of vitality on the probability of the Court negatively interpreting a precedent when the Court and the precedent are ideologically distant from one another.

To further illustrate these propositions, we again plot three possible scenarios consistents with our theoretical model (see figure 2.2). The only difference across these scenarios is the relative magnitudes of b_7 (the effect of vitality corresponding with the benefit derived from altering existing precedent) and b_8 (the effect of vitality corresponding with the legitimacy cost associated with negative interpretation).

In the first scenario, b_7 is larger in magnitude than b_8, and this leads the effect of precedent vitality to switch directions at some value of ideological distance. Precedent vitality exerts a negative effect on the utility (and thus probability) of interpreting a precedent negatively when ideological distance is low and exerts a positive effect for high values of ideological distance. In the third scenario, b_8 is larger in magnitude than b_7, causing high vitality precedents to always be less likely to be interpreted negatively than their low vitality counterparts. The second scenario depicts the utilities when b_7 and b_8 are of equal magnitude. For all three scenarios, increases in ideological distance lead to increases in the utility associated with treating a precedent negatively (Proposition 2.5), and this effect is stronger for highly vital precedents (Proposition 2.6). In addition, each scenario indicates that the justices receive less utility from negatively interpreting more vital precedents which are ideologically compatible with their policy goals (Proposition 2.6).

In the empirical chapters that follow, we can estimate $-(b_7 + b_8)$ and thus empirically establish the relative strength of the legitimacy incentive aspect of vitality relative to the policy incentive aspect. When doing so, we will be able to compare the empirical relationships we find with the hypothetical scenarios presented in figure 2.2.

SUMMARY OF ARGUMENT AND EXPECTATIONS

We posit that the decision to interpret precedent is driven by the desire to influence the scope and meaning of existing precedent and the goal of legitimizing new legal policy. Both of these motivations, we argue, relate to the justices' overarching goal of setting policy that will ultimately lead to the outcomes they desire. We thus expect the decision to interpret precedent to be affected by the ideological distance between the sitting justices and the precedent, the vitality of the precedent, and the interaction between these two variables. Precedent vitality should attenuate or dampen the negative effect of ideological distance on the probability of positive interpretation and accentuate the positive effect of ideological distance on the likelihood of negative treatment.

This theoretical model is distinct from existing discussions of precedent. Prior research typically characterizes precedent as an exogenous constraint on the Court that either exists (e.g., Aldisert 1990; Schauer 1987) or does not exist (e.g., Segal and Spaeth 1993, 2002). The latter tradition implies either that the Court would not be bothered to interpret precedent at all or that the interpretation of precedent is solely a function of the ideological compatibility of the precedent with the interpreting Court. It is not clear exactly what the former theoretical tradition implies regarding the interpretation of precedent, but it would seem to exclude any role for the policy preferences of the justices.

Our theory of *stare decisis* focuses on precedent vitality, which pertains to the reach and legal authority of a case. We argue that the vitality of precedent can both provide an opportunity for the Court (in terms of influencing extant legal policy) and represent a constraint on the Court's choices (in terms of needing to legitimize new legal policy). Our theory thus points toward a new way of understanding the role of precedent at the Court. The treatment of precedent is not simply a function of the compatibility between a precedent and the Court or the result of highly constrained judicial choices. Instead, precedent vitality combines with judicial policy preferences to determine how precedent will be interpreted over time. More specifically, precedent vitality acts to condition the effect of the ideological distance between the Court and the policy established by a precedent.

THEORETICAL ISSUES AND LIMITATIONS

Critical readers may raise several questions or issues regarding the theoretical framework we have proposed. Along the way, we have tried to address several potential criticisms. In this section, we anticipate and address two remaining issues.

Parsimony vs. Comprehensive Explanation

When attempting to explain something as complex as the determinants of the Supreme Court's interpretation of precedent, there is a trade-off to be made between parsimony and comprehensive explanation (see Baum 1997). The model we presented above clearly falls toward the parsimony end of this continuum. We simplify reality and in the process ignore (or at least deemphasize) factors that other scholars may see as relevant. Rather than viewing this as a limitation, we see it as one of our principal strengths (see King, Keohane, and Verba 1994, 19–20). By presenting a model built on the most fundamental aspects of the phenomenon we seek to explain, we provide a tightly focused explanation and generate precise empirical predictions.

Nevertheless, we recognize the need to control for factors that do not derive from our theoretical framework when estimating our empirical models. Their presence in our statistical models controls for alternative explanations, allowing us to draw confident inferences from the empirical results for our theoretical variables of interest. These control variables can be divided into two groups.

The first set is comprised of precedent characteristics that prior research suggests influence subsequent interpretations. The literature specifically suggests that separate opinions and smaller decision coalitions will cause a precedent to be weaker and thus less likely to be interpreted positively and more likely to be interpreted negatively (e.g., Aldisert 1990, 632; Danelski 1986; Johnson 1979, 1987; Peczenik 1997). We therefore include in our empirical models control variables for the number of concurring opinions accompanying a precedent and the size of the decision coalition in a precedent.

The second set of control variables contains factors that influence whether a precedent is likely to be interpreted at all by the Court. These variables may affect the extent to which the precedent either is salient or remains relevant for contemporary legal problems. In other words, these are considerations that may explain why a precedent receives subsequent interpretations but will not explain the type of interpretation accorded to it. Examples of this kind of control variable include the following. A precedent whose issue area remains active on the Court's agenda is more likely to be interpreted. Precedents dealing with a larger number and range of legal issues are also more likely to receive Court treatment. We control for these and several other considerations that affect the likelihood of a precedent being interpreted in our empirical models. In a sense, we opt for parsimony when developing our theoretical model but err on the side of comprehensive explanation when estimating our statistical models. Greater detail regarding these control variables is provided in chapter 4.

A Theory for the U.S. Supreme Court

Our theory of the interpretation of precedent applies to the U.S. Supreme Court. While the broader ideas driving our theory most likely apply across a wide variety of courts, differences in their institutional features (e.g., degree of discretionary docket control, potential for review by a higher court) would necessitate alterations to the model. For example, a trial court judge cannot hope to have as much influence as the Supreme Court over how a wide range of decision makers use a precedent. Appeals court panels can affect the applicability and vitality of a precedent to some extent, but may be constrained in how they treat a precedent by the possibility of Supreme Court review. It is important to understand how and why lower court judges use or interpret precedent (see Comparato and McClurg 2003), but to do so would require theoretical modifications that are outside the scope of this study.

CHAPTER THREE

Measuring the Interpretation of Precedent

BEFORE TURNING to our empirical assessments of the propositions presented in chapter 2, we need to discuss the data we will be using. The precedents examined in this book include all Supreme Court cases (orally argued full opinions, *per curiams*, and judgments of the Court) decided between the 1946 and 1999 terms of the Court.[1] This designation results in 6,363 Supreme Court precedents.[2] Our objective is to explain when and why the Court subsequently interprets these cases positively or negatively.

To answer the questions posed in prior chapters, we require data on the Court's positive and negative interpretation of its precedents, starting in the year a case was decided and ending in 2001. Developing such measures for a large number of Court precedents over a significant period of time is no easy task. One reason is that they require careful content analysis of every Supreme Court opinion decided over a time span of more than 50 years in order to determine which precedents the Court positively or negatively treats. Consequently, one confronts both a large number of cases and a subjective, and potentially difficult, task of classifying the Court's treatment of precedent. The scope of this measurement task is one reason why scholars typically study the ideological outcome of cases or the individual justices' votes on the merits.

Fortunately, there is an existing source of data that nicely matches our measurement needs. To develop indicators of the positive and negative interpretation of each case, we use *Shepard's Citations*. *Shepard's* is a legal citation index that, among other things, provides a list of all U.S.

[1] We recognize that while we equate a Supreme Court decision with a Supreme Court precedent, some decisions may create multiple legal rules. An alternative approach would be to define each specific legal rule as being an individual precedent. The problem with this approach is that while a Supreme Court decision is a tidy unit of analysis, it would be difficult to reliably classify multiple precedents within a decision. Moreover, *Shepard's Citations* provides subsequent court interpretations of a court decision, not specific legal rules within that decision. Perhaps the main issue with allowing a precedent to consist of multiple legal rules is that precedents establishing multiple legal rules may be more likely to be interpreted in the future. We have a control variable (*Breadth of Precedent*, which we will discuss in chapter 4), however, that captures this feature of a precedent.

[2] We gathered these data from Spaeth (1995, 2001) using case citation as the unit of analysis, excluding the 67 cases for which Spaeth coded the case outcome as non-ideological.

court opinions that refer to any U.S. state or federal court case decided since the beginning of the U.S. legal system. Importantly, *Shepard's* also indicates how a particular court opinion is legally interpreted by the subsequently decided cases that cite it.

In this chapter, we first acquaint the reader with the protocols *Shepard's* employs to collect its data. We then empirically analyze the reliability of *Shepard's* data and discuss their validity for our study. Finally, we present aggregate data regarding the way in which the U.S. Supreme Court has legally interpreted the Supreme Court precedents in our analysis. The presentation of this information serves as a transition to chapters 4 through 6, where we directly test our hypotheses regarding the Supreme Court's interpretation of precedent.

THE DATA COLLECTION PROTOCOLS OF *SHEPARD'S CITATIONS*

For each published state and federal court case decided since the beginning of the U.S. legal system (which we refer to as a precedent), *Shepard's* provides a list of all subsequently decided cases which refer to it (which we term treatment cases). *Shepard's* also analyzes how the treatment case legally interprets the precedent.[3] The question *Shepard's* asks in each case is the following: "What effect, if any, does the citing [treatment] case have on the cited case [precedent]?" (Shepard's 1993, 13). *Shepard's* goal is to "verify the current status of each case in order to establish whether it is still effective law, or has been reversed, overruled, or its authority has been otherwise diminished" (Shepard's 1993, 2).

We conceptualize the interpretation of precedent as being either positive or negative, and we therefore need measures of each. *Shepard's* data are nicely suited for our needs in that its categorization of the treatment of precedent falls into these very categories of positive and negative treatment.[4] Importantly, *Shepard's* has developed a coding scheme (contained in an unpublished training manual) that explicitly lays out rules

---

[3] *Shepard's* provides the editorial analysis for a treatment case's majority and concurring opinions, while for a dissenting opinion *Shepard's* only notes whether it refers to a previously decided case. *Shepard's* has only recently begun noting in its data whether a particular treatment is in a majority or concurring opinion. We checked all the treatments to ensure that we were only collecting data from majority opinions.

[4] *Shepard's* also presents a third, residual category that does not constitute either positive or negative interpretation of a precedent. This category of neutral treatments contains two of *Shepard's* treatment codes: (1) "Explained" indicates that "the citing opinion clarifies, interprets, construes or otherwise annotates the decision in the cited case" (Shepard's 1993, 16); and (2) "Harmonized" means "that the cases differ in some way; however, the court has found a way to reconcile and bring into harmony the apparent inconsistency" (Shepard's 1993, 18).

for determining whether an opinion treats a precedent either positively or negatively. More specifically, *Shepard's* coding scheme includes one treatment category that can be considered as positive interpretation and five that relate to negative interpretation. *Shepard's* labels a positive interpretation of a precedent as "Followed." The treatments that *Shepard's* labels as "Distinguished," "Criticized," "Limited," "Questioned," and "Overruled" denote the negative interpretation of a precedent. In order for *Shepard's* to apply one of these treatments to a precedent, the treatment opinion must do more than simply cite it. The treatment case must provide specific language that has a potential effect on the legal authority of the precedent (Shepard's 1993, 13). As we show below, these rules lead to data that are replicable and valid.

Let us first discuss the positive interpretation of precedent. *Shepard's* considers a precedent as being positively interpreted if the treatment case follows the precedent, meaning the treatment case cited the precedent as "controlling authority" (Shepard's 1993, 17). We therefore deem a precedent as being positively treated by the Court when Shepard's codes a majority opinion (again, orally argued full opinion, *per curiam*, or judgment of the Court) as treating a precedent by *Following* it.[5]

For *Shepard's* to conclude that a precedent has been positively treated in a subsequent opinion, the opinion must "in some firm way refer to the cited case [precedent] as compelling precedent" (Shepard's 1993, 17). As *Shepard's* training manual for its employees indicates: "A mere 'going-along' with the cited case [precedent] would not be sufficient for assigning a letter 'f' ["Follow"]. . . . Merely citing or quoting, with nothing more, is not a sufficient expression of reliance to permit an 'f' (Or any letter, for that matter)" (Shepard's 1993, 17). Examples of language in an opinion that indicate positive treatment include: " 'controlling,' 'applicable,' 'determinative,' 'persuasive' "; "We affirm on the authority of . . . , or on the teaching of . . . , or for the reasons stated in . . . or under the rationale of . . ."; Such a conclusion is required by . . . or governed by . . ."; "We see no reason to depart from the holding in . . ." (Shepard's 1993, 17).

Shepard's codes a treatment case as negatively interpreting a precedent if specific language in the treatment opinion exerts a negative effect on the legal authority of the precedent (Shepard's 1993, 14, 24). Within this

---

[5] There are four instances across this time period in which *Shepard's* uses the treatment category of "Parallel," meaning that the treatment case "states that the cited case [precedent] is identical, on all fours, or parallel in its facts or in the law or both" (Shepard's 1993, 21). According to John Strand (phone conversation on 11-10-98), a Shepard's employee, Parallel is no longer used as a treatment category, and instead such cases are coded as Followed. Since these four Parallel treatments are effectively the same as a Follow, we include them in our measure of positive interpretation.

category of negative treatment, *Shepard's* utilizes five different treatment designations—Overrule, Question, Limit, Criticize, and Distinguish. We therefore consider any one of these treatments in a majority opinion (again, orally argued full opinion, *per curiam*, or judgment of the Court) as a negative interpretation of a precedent.[6]

Shepard's training manual is replete with examples of language signaling negative interpretation. We will provide a few to give the reader a flavor for what they look like. "The holding of this case is now of limited application . . ."; "The Rule in 'X v. Y' shall be limited [or confined] to its own set of facts . . ."; "We refuse to extend the rule of 'C v. D' to this situation . . ."; " 'A v. B' has no bearing on this case . . ."; "We think this case is wrong and respectfully decline to follow it . . ."; "The reasoning of A v. B has been rendered invalid by C v. D and its progeny . . ."; "We do not find 'In Re Smith' applicable to the instant situation . . ." (Shepard's 1993, 14–22). Again, each of these phrases, and others discussed in the *Shepard's* training manual, point out that a Court opinion in some way diminishes the reach of a precedent or at least explicitly lays out why the case is inapposite for a dispute.

The Reliability of Shepard's Citations

The Shepard's Company, which publishes *Shepard's Citations*, hires and trains attorneys to content-analyze court opinions, a process it terms "letter editing." These letter editors receive extensive training based in part on the coding rules set forth in an in-house, unpublished training manual. This manual includes nearly 25 single-spaced pages of material on the overall letter-editing process, with 13 pages strictly devoted to laying out the coding rules for the treatment categories (Shepard's 1993, 1–25). Thus, Shepard's recognizes the subjective nature of the coding enterprise and has developed coding rules to try and maximize data reliability.

It is essential that we show empirically that these coding rules lead to reliable data, or data that are reproducible (Carmines and Zeller 1979). Because the strength of a study's results ultimately depends in part on the accuracy of the data, we empirically tested the reliability of *Shepard's Citation*'s analysis of Supreme Court opinions. Our results indicate that

---

[6] We exclude from negative interpretation any Questioned code that did not truly interpret the precedent. Specifically, we did not count as negative interpretation any Questioned treatment that simply noted that some prior Court opinion or legislative enactment overturned the precedent without actually negatively interpreting the precedent itself. The reason we drop these treatments is because they do not actually interpret the precedent. To make this determination, we read each treatment case that *Shepard's* coded as Questioning a precedent.

Shepard's data on the positive and negative interpretation of precedent are highly reliable.

Our replication proceeds in three steps. First, we determined whether *Shepard's* failed to list cases actually cited in Court opinions. More specifically, we ascertained whether, for 25 randomly selected Supreme Court treatment cases, *Shepard's* excluded any of the precedents cited in them. Using the *United States Supreme Court Reports—Lawyer's Edition*, we located 300 precedents in these 25 randomly selected opinions. We then "shepardized" each of these 300 cases to ascertain whether *Shepard's* listed it as being cited by the treatment case. As one might expect (given the nonsubjective nature of this coding decision), this aspect of *Shepard's* data is exceptionally reliable. Indeed, we find that *Shepard's* had an accuracy rate of 100% in that it included each of the precedents as being referenced in the 25 treatment cases. Thus, we conclude that *Shepard's* list of precedents is most likely not underinclusive.[7]

Second, for each treatment case *Shepard's* must determine whether the precedent is legally interpreted (i.e., either treated positively or negatively) by the treatment opinion or is just cited without any substantive legal treatment. For *Shepard's* to designate that a precedent was positively or negatively treated, the treatment case must contain language that explicitly exerts a potential influence on the reach of the precedent (Shepard's 1993, 2, 13). A mere string citation, for example, would not by itself warrant a treatment code, and such a case would be listed in *Shepard's* as citing, though not legally interpreting, the precedent. We

---

[7] Songer (1988) suggests two other reasons that Shepard's may be underinclusive. First, he indicates that *Shepard's* only lists a case if the court opinion gives the full citation. According to Shepard's personnel (phone conversations with Leslie Martin 6-8-98, Rebecca Marshall 6-30-98, and John Strand 9-13-99) this is not accurate. They indicated that *Shepard's* includes any case that is referenced in an opinion, regardless of whether the full cite is given. If the full cite to a case is not given, Shepard's employees indicated to us that they make every effort to ascertain to which case the court opinion refers. In fact, they keep a list of popular names court opinions will sometimes use when referring to another case, such as "Erie Doctrine" or "Frye standard." Most importantly, *Shepard's* policy is to include references to *cases*, and they will not include a reference to a *doctrine* without a reference to the case. For example, if a court simply refers to the "Miranda rights," without referring to the case at some point in the opinion, then *Shepard's* will not list the case. Nevertheless, we do not anticipate this issue to pose a problem at the U.S. Supreme Court, because in our experience the Court almost always provides full citations to a cited case somewhere in the citing opinion. Second, Songer (1988) suggests that if a court defies a precedent, and thus does not refer to the precedent when it should, *Shepard's* will not list the case. We think it unlikely that the Supreme Court would systematically fail to cite precedents that are directly relevant for a case. Indeed, it would be difficult to even determine when the Court should cite a case, given the complexity, novelty, and disagreement surrounding most Supreme Court cases.

must therefore ascertain whether *Shepard's* reliably determines when a treatment case legally treats a precedent.

To do so, we randomly selected 25 U.S. Supreme Court cases decided between 1946 and 1987.[8] We then used Boolean word searches in Lexis for the litigant names and case citations to locate every subsequent Supreme Court opinion (through January 1999) referring to each of these 25 cases. This procedure resulted in a sample of 252 potential treatment cases for these 25 precedents. We then read each potential treatment opinion, coding it as either legally treating the precedent or just mentioning it without any substantive treatment. Our coding agrees with *Shepard's* 88.5% of the time, for a Kappa statistic of .683 (p < .001).[9] This statistic means that the level of agreement is 68.3% greater than would be expected by chance and thus indicates "substantial" intercoder agreement (see Cohen 1960; Landis and Koch 1977).[10] Therefore, *Shepard's* designation of substantive legal treatment, as opposed to a mere case citation, appears to be reliable.

Third, for each Supreme Court case decided between the 1946 and 1995 terms we used *Shepard's* to identify all subsequent cases that positively or negatively treated it.[11] To replicate *Shepard's* coding of the treatment cases' positive or negative interpretation of the precedents, we took a 6% random stratified sample (N = 602) of all the treatment cases in

[8] We used 1987 as an end date to ensure that each precedent had enough time to be cited by the Court in subsequently decided cases.

[9] While our sample is relatively small (N = 252), given the amount of time it takes to code these cases the 95% confidence interval around the Kappa is a reasonably tight ± .121.

[10] Kappa = $(p_o - p_c)/(1 - p_c)$, where p_o is the observed proportion of agreement, and p_c is the proportion of agreement expected by chance (Cohen 1968). The Kappa statistic can range from below zero to one. If Kappa equals zero, then the amount of agreement between the two coders is exactly what one would expect by chance. If Kappa equals one, then the coders agree perfectly. When evaluating the extent to which the two coders agree, Landis and Koch (1977) attach the following labels to the size of the Kappa statistic: < 0.00 is "Poor"; 0.00–0.20 is "Slight"; 0.21–0.40 is "Fair"; 0.41–0.60 is "Moderate"; 0.61–0.80 is "Substantial"; and 0.81–1.00 is "Almost Perfect."

[11] Our reliability data end in 1995, not 2001, because we conducted the reliability analysis toward the beginning of this project when our data ended in 1995. We have since gathered data through 2001, and we see no reason why the reliability of the 1996–2001 treatments would be different from the 1946–1995 treatments. In fact, one might be concerned that the opposite would be true—that the older data are less reliable—because there have been some changes to *Shepard's* coding protocols over time. We, of course, use the modern coding protocols when testing the reliability of the older *Shepard's* data. To check the robustness of the reliability scores over time, we split the data in half, and analyzed treatments prior to and after 1975. We do not find that the earlier data are less reliable. Specifically, the Kappa for positive treatment before 1975 is .645, and it is .622 for the post-1975 period; the Kappas, pre- and post-1975 respectively, are .680 and .733 for negative interpretation.

Shepard's for this time period.[12] We then read all of the treatment cases' majority opinions in the *U.S. Reports*, coding how each treatment opinion legally treated the precedents cited in it using the coding rules located in the *Shepard's* (1993) in-house training manual. Our analysis indicates that the categories of positive and negative interpretation are quite reliable. The intercoder agreement for the negative treatment code is 86.1%, and the Kappa statistic is .718.[13] The positive treatment category also falls within Landis and Koch's substantial agreement classification, with a Kappa statistic of .628 (82.7% agreement).

The Validity of Shepard's Citations

We now wish to consider the validity of *Shepard's* data for measuring the positive and negative interpretation of precedent. Validity refers to the idea that a variable should actually capture the concept it is intended to measure (see Carmines and Zeller 1979). There is no formal statistical test we can use for testing the validity of these data, and we therefore discuss their face validity.

The core, commercial purpose of *Shepard's Citations* is to provide lawyers and judges with information about the legal authority of a case. *Shepard's* has been providing this service for about 60 years, and its use in the legal community is standard practice. Indeed, *Shepard's* states that the function of its data is precisely what we want to measure: "what effect, if any, does the citing case [treatment case] have on the cited case [precedent]" (Shepard's 1993, 13). Given the role of precedent in our legal system, *Shepard's* provides these data so that interested parties can discern whether, after a precedent is interpreted, it is "still good authority" (Shepard's 1993, 1). Thus, the way in which we use *Shepard's* data is entirely consistent with the purpose for which they are gathered.

---

[12] We use the aggregated categories of positive and negative interpretation in this book (and thus focus on their reliability), but elsewhere we also tested the reliability of the individual treatment categories (see Spriggs and Hansford 2000). Given this broader goal, we used a stratified sample because it is the most appropriate way to ensure that all of the individual treatment categories were adequately represented in the reliability data (see Krippendorff 1980, 146). This sampling design was appropriate, since a number of the individual treatment categories do not occur very frequently. While Overruled, Questioned, Criticized, Limited, and Harmonized respectively occur in only .6%, 2.5%, 1.3%, .2%, and 1.3% of treatment cases' interpretations of precedents decided in the 1946–1995 terms, they respectively comprise 2.8%, 7.8%, 5.7%, 2.0%, and 4.7% of our reliability sample. We did not conduct a reliability analysis of the Parallel code because *Shepard's* applied it only four times during this entire time period.

[13] The Kappa statistics for the individual treatment codes on which negative interpretation is based are the following: Overrule .907; Question .713; Limited .781; Criticized .618; Distinguished .678.

Moreover, we use *Shepard's* in much the same way that lawyers, judges, and their clerks use it—to ascertain whether subsequent Court decisions have altered the meaning and reach of a Court precedent.

There are two limitations of *Shepard's* for this study that we need to discuss, however. The first issue is that *Shepard's* coding rules require a treatment case to contain *explicit* language in order for a treatment code to be applied. This feature of the data results in an important advantage, namely, the reliability of the data, but it also leads to a disadvantage: it may result in *Shepard's* occasionally not acknowledging that an interpretation of a precedent exists when the court treats it without *explicitly* indicating that it does so. To the extent that this occurs, our dependent variables may be somewhat underinclusive.

A second issue is the potential for heterogeneity within negative interpretation. We are theoretically interested in positive and negative interpretation, but *Shepard's* coding scheme does distinguish between "strong" negative interpretation (Overrule, Question, Limit, and Criticize) and "weak" negative interpretation (Distinguish) (Shepard's 1993, 23–24). Distinguished may at times represent a somewhat weaker form of negative interpretation than the others because, while at a minimum it indicates that a case is inapplicable, it may not necessarily restrict the application of the precedent. By contrast, the other four types of negative interpretation are stronger, according to *Shepard's*, because they likely undercut the value of the precedent in more significant ways. To ensure that our results for negative interpretation are consistent across these potentially different forms of negative treatments, the analysis presented in chapter 4 is conducted in two ways: for all types of negative interpretation, and for the weaker form of negative interpretation (i.e., Distinguished) alone. In addition, given the relative importance and salience of the overruling of precedent, chapter 5 focuses on this particularly strong form of negative interpretation.

In short, we contend that the data we use from *Shepard's* are valid and reliable indicators of positive and negative interpretation. We have empirically demonstrated that they are replicable. We recognize that our measures are not perfect and acknowledge that they have certain limitations. We nonetheless believe that they are currently the best data available for measuring the positive and negative interpretation of precedent across a large sample of court cases.

Aggregate Trends in the Interpretation of Precedent

Let us now turn to a brief look at the incidence of the Court's treatment of its previously decided cases (see table 3.1). Our data indicate that of

TABLE 3.1

The Frequency with Which Precedents Decided between the 1946 and 1999 Terms Have Been Interpreted by the Supreme Court through 2001

Number of Times Interpreted	Positively		Negatively		Positively or Negatively	
	Number of Precedents (Percentage)		Number of Precedents (Percentage)		Number of Precedents (Percentage)	
0	4,402	(69.2)	4,212	(66.2)	3,300	(51.9)
1	1,265	(19.9)	1,271	(20.0)	1,458	(22.9)
2	384	(6.0)	516	(8.1)	733	(11.5)
3	150	(2.4)	194	(3.0)	329	(5.2)
4	70	(1.1)	87	(1.4)	205	(3.2)
5	34	(.5)	45	(.7)	124	(2.0)
6	17	(.3)	16	(.3)	78	(1.2)
7	14	(.2)	11	(.2)	37	(.6)
8	5	(.08)	5	(.08)	30	(.5)
9	6	(.08)	3	(.05)	20	(.3)
10	4	(.06)	2	(.03)	11	(.2)
11	2	(.03)	0	(0)	9	(.1)
12	3	(.05)	0	(0)	4	(.06)
13	3	(.05)	1	(.02)	8	(.1)
14 or more	4	(.06)	0	(0)	17	(.26)
Total	6,363 (100.01)		6,363 (100.08)		6,363 (100.02)	

Note: Cell entries represent the number (percentage) of precedents established between the 1946 and 1999 terms of the Court that experienced the relevant number of interpretations by 2001. The authors collected these data from Shepard's Citations.

the 6,363 precedents decided between the 1946 and 1999 terms of the Court, the Court subsequently interpreted 3,063 (48.1%) by the end of 2001. Approximately 31% (1,961) of these precedents received positive interpretation by the Court, while 34% (2,151) of them were negatively interpreted. In addition, the Court exclusively interpreted about 14% (912) of these precedents positively and interpreted another 17.3% (1,102) of them only negatively. Finally, the Court interpreted 16.5% (1,049) of these precedents both positively and negatively over this time span.

The frequency with which the Court interpreted a precedent either positively or negatively ranged from a low of 0 to a high of 23. A majority of cases (51.9%) have not yet been legally treated by the Court. Most cases that were interpreted garnered one, two, or three treatments by the Court over the study's time frame. Few cases received more than five legal treatments by the Court, with only 3.4% of cases falling in this range of the data.

It is also instructive to disaggregate these data into the number of positive and negative treatments of precedent. The total number of positive treatments for this time period varied from 0 to 20 per precedent, and the range for negative interpretation was 0 to 13.[14] Most precedents that the Court interpreted were either positively or negatively treated by the Court on one occasion. The respective average numbers of positive and negative interpretations per case over this time period are .54 and .59. There are, however, a minority of cases that received multiple Court treatments. The Court, for instance, interpreted 3.0%, 1.4%, and 0.7% of its precedents negatively three, four, or five different times.[15]

It is important to recognize that these frequencies are pushed downward a bit because more recently decided cases have not had long to be treated by the Court. For precedents that were ten years or older by 2001, 52.3% have been interpreted either positively or negatively by the Court. This percentage is considerably higher than that for cases younger than ten years, for which fewer than 21% have been interpreted by the Court. Thus, while the above numbers provide important information, they do not capture an important aspect of legal treatment, its timing.

With regard to the issue of timing, Richard Fenno (1986, 9) once observed that "We have devoted more energy to studying policy positioning in space than to studying policy sequencing in time. To our rich comprehension of the politics of left, right, and center, we can usefully add an equally rich comprehension of the politics of early, later, and late." This idea applies with force to this research for two reasons. First, the question at the heart of this study is how law develops. To understand this issue, we should therefore study patterns in the law over time. Thus, our dependent variable must take into account the timing and sequencing of the interpretation of precedent. Second, our theory of the interpretation of precedent is dynamic in character. Our two key theoretical in-

---

[14] The three most actively interpreted precedents by the Court were *Miranda v. Arizona* (1966), *Lemon v. Kurtzman* (1971), and *Mathews v. Eldridge* (1976). *Miranda* also ranks as the case receiving the greatest number of negative interpretations, while *Lemon* received the greatest number of positive treatments by the Court.

[15] We note that a handful of precedents are not garnering the bulk of treatments. Of the cases that are interpreted, most only receive one or two treatments. These data demonstrate that there is a considerable amount of variation in our dependent variables. To make sure that cases with a large number of treatments are not driving our results, we estimated our empirical models after censoring cases with multiple interpretations. The results indicate that this censoring has little effect on our results. We therefore conclude that our results are not being driven by the cases that have been heavily interpreted.

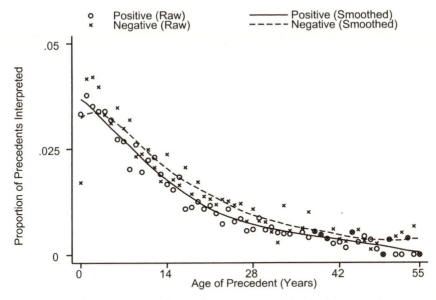

Figure 3.1. The proportion of precedents interpreted by the Supreme Court over time

Note: The authors gathered these data from *Shepard's Citations.*

dependent variables—the ideological distance between the Court and a precedent and the legal vitality of a precedent—both capture important changes in the Court and a precedent over time. In order to test our theory, then, we must examine the empirical patterns in the timing of the Court's treatment of its precedents.

To get a sense for the likelihood of a precedent being interpreted over time, figure 3.1 provides data on the proportion of precedents interpreted positively and negatively in a given year of a precedent's "life." Both the raw proportions and lowess-smoothed plots of these proportions are included in the figure.

What is immediately evident is that the proportion of precedents interpreted either positively or negatively in a given year is low. Another obvious feature of these data is that the frequency of positive and negative interpretations significantly declines as a precedent ages. While, for instance, 3.8% of precedents are interpreted positively by the Court when they are one year old, this percentage drops to 0.8% and .004% for precedents that are 25 or 50 years old, respectively.

In summary, the Court's interpretation of its precedents is not a frequent event. Once decided, many cases are not subsequently treated by the Court. The modal precedent decided from the 1946 through 1999 terms had not yet been legally treated by 2001, and the average precedent had received one legal interpretation. There is, however, meaningful variation in the incidence of legal treatment. While the Court interpreted nearly 23% of cases on one occasion, it respectively treated 3.2% and 2% four or five times, and another 3.4% gathered more than five treatments. Because of the important legal and political consequences that can result from the treatment of precedent, we argue that, despite its low rate of occurrence, it is a centrally important part of Court behavior. We also argue that this behavior is systematic and predictable, being driven by the dynamics described in chapter 2. In the next three chapters, we turn to empirical tests of the predictions from our model.

Conclusion

This chapter set out to define our dependent variable and provide descriptive data on its frequency and timing. We measure positive and negative treatment using *Shepard's Citations*, which indicates how treatment cases legally interpret precedents. These data are well suited for our purpose because they fall into the conceptual categories of interest, positive and negative interpretation of precedent. We fully recognize that one hallmark of good social science is ensuring that data are replicable, and we therefore empirically established the reliability of *Shepard's* data. We also considered the validity of our data, concluding that, with some caveats, *Shepard's* data match well with our idea of positive and negative interpretation.

Our presentation of descriptive data on our dependent variable offers the reader an initial sense of how it varies across cases and over time. Importantly, there is variation both in the number and timing of these legal treatments. This variation is precisely what we intend to explain. Our argument is that the presence and timing of these legal treatments depends crucially on our two explanatory variables—the ideological distance between a case and the Court, and the legal vitality of a case—and the interaction between these two variables. Thus, while legal treatment of prior cases is a somewhat infrequent event at the Court, subsequent chapters will show that it is both predictable and important.

CHAPTER FOUR

The Interpretation of Precedent over Time

AFTER BEING CONVICTED of felony possession of marijuana, a California man requested that the appellate court appoint him an attorney so that he could appeal his conviction. The court appointed an attorney, who turned around and wrote a letter to the court stating that he would not appeal the case because he was " 'of the opinion that there is no merit to the appeal' " (386 U.S. 738, 742). The appeals court then affirmed the conviction and the defendant ultimately appealed to the U.S. Supreme Court. In this case, *Anders v. California* (1967), the Warren Court ruled that court-appointed attorneys cannot, against their client's wishes, simply decline to file the first appeal of a criminal conviction. A court-appointed attorney must "support his client's appeal to the best of his ability" (386 U.S. 738, 744).[1] For court-appointed attorneys facing truly meritless appeals, the Court established a specific, safeguard-filled procedure to follow in order to withdraw from an appeal. Essentially, this precedent sought to make it less likely that a court-appointed attorney might decline to appeal a case that actually had some legal merit.

More than three decades later, the Rehnquist Court negatively interpreted the *Anders* precedent in *Smith v. Robbins* (2000). The Court held that the specific procedures for a court-appointed attorney to decline to appeal a criminal conviction set forth in *Anders* are, more or less, suggestions, not requirements. States may adopt other procedures, as long as they make sure that defendants have adequate access to legal counsel. Even though procedures being used in California still did not meet what appeared to be the *Anders* standard, the Court found them to be constitutional. As implied in the dissenting opinions, the *Smith* majority's treatment of *Anders* reduced its effectiveness and made it easier for states to allow court-appointed attorneys to decline to represent defendants appealing criminal convictions. Depending upon your perspective, the negative interpretation of *Anders* either made the criminal justice

---

[1] The majority opinion did note, however, that a court-appointed attorney could request permission to withdraw from the case, if the case was absolutely without merit. The attorney must still provide the court with a brief supporting the appeal, though.

system more efficient by reducing frivolous appeals, or undercut procedural protections designed to ensure that poor criminal defendants receive the same quality of legal representation as those who can afford their own attorney.

This chapter is the first of three in which we utilize the data discussed in chapter 3 to test specific hypotheses derived from the general theoretical expectations laid out in chapter 2. In this chapter, we address the following questions: (1) when will a Supreme Court precedent be interpreted positively by the Court in a given year; and (2) when will a precedent be interpreted negatively? To put this second question in terms of the substantive example above, why did the Rehnquist Court negatively treat *Anders* in 2000? We test six hypotheses about the interpretation of precedent over time by analyzing the Court's subsequent interpretation of the precedents it established from the 1946 through 1999 terms. This chapter thus presents a systematic empirical examination of how Supreme Court precedents evolve over the years, as the Court treats them positively or negatively.

Hypotheses

We argued in chapter 2 that the justices' motivation to interpret precedent derives from both the desire to impact the body of existing legal precedent and the need to legitimize new policy choices. The former incentive leads the justices to treat a precedent based on the interaction between its compatibility with their policy preferences and the legal vitality of the precedent (i.e., the legal authority of a case, as determined by the Court's prior interpretation of it). The latter incentive encourages justices to make choices about how to interpret precedent solely based on its legal vitality. Thus, the Court's interpretation of precedent depends on the interplay between the compatibility of a precedent with the justices' policy preferences and the legal vitality of the precedent. To be a bit more precise, we expect the decision to interpret precedent to be a function of the ideological distance between the sitting justices and the precedent, the vitality of the precedent, and the interaction between these two variables. Precedent vitality will attenuate the negative effect of ideological distance on the probability of positive interpretation and amplify the positive effect of ideological distance on the likelihood of negative treatment.

Based on this argument, we developed six propositions, three for the positive interpretation of precedent and three for negative interpretation. Each of these six general propositions leads to a specific prediction regarding the probability of the Supreme Court interpreting a particular precedent positively or negatively in a given year.

Hypothesis 4.1: *The greater the ideological distance between a precedent and the Court in year* y *(i.e., a given year), the smaller the probability that the Court will positively interpret the precedent in that year (see Proposition 2.1).*

Hypothesis 4.2: *The more vital the precedent is in year* y, *the smaller the negative effect of ideological distance on the probability of positive treatment in that year (see Proposition 2.2).*

Hypothesis 4.3: *The vitality of a precedent in year* y *will exert a positive effect on the probability of the precedent being interpreted positively in year* y, *if the precedent is ideologically distant from the Court (see Proposition 2.3).*

Hypothesis 4.4: *The greater the ideological distance between a precedent and the Court in year* y, *the greater the probability that the Court will negatively interpret the precedent in year* y *(see Proposition 2.4).*

Hypothesis 4.5: *The more vital a precedent is in year* y, *the larger the positive effect of ideological distance on the probability of negative interpretation in that year (see Proposition 2.5).*

Hypothesis 4.6: *The vitality of a precedent in year* y *will exert a negative effect on the probability of the precedent being interpreted negatively in year* y, *if the precedent is ideologically close to the Court (see Proposition 2.6).*

In short, the Supreme Court will positively treat precedents that closely reflect the Court's preferences and will negatively treat precedents that are ideologically incongruent with the Court. Importantly, precedent vitality conditions these relationships, however, by decreasing the effect of ideological distance on the likelihood of positive interpretation and increasing the effect of ideological distance on the probability of negative interpretation. Based on our theory, the direct or main effect of precedent vitality on the likelihood of positive or negative interpretation can only be predicted for specific ranges of values of ideological distance.

Data and Measurement

Dependent Variables

To examine empirically the U.S. Supreme Court's interpretation of a precedent in a given year, we utilize the universe of the Court's orally argued opinions decided from the 1946 through 1999 terms.[2] As described in chapter 3, we use *Shepard's Citations* to identify every Supreme Court majority opinion, decided by the end of 2001, which subsequently interpreted one of these 6,363 precedents. More specifically, we use *Shepard's Citations* to determine when one of the Court's majority opinions positively or negatively interpreted each of the precedents in our data. Following *Shepard's*, we consider any treatment case that "Followed" a precedent as positively interpreting that precedent. We code any situation in which the Court "Distinguished," "Criticized," "Limited," "Questioned," or "Overruled" a precedent as negative interpretation.[3]

The precise questions we address in this chapter are the following: In a given year, how likely is the U.S. Supreme Court to interpret a given precedent positively, and how likely is it to interpret the precedent negatively? To test our hypotheses regarding these questions, we use a dataset containing an observation for each precedent in each year of its existence, beginning in the year it was decided and ending in 2001. For example, we have 35 observations for *Anders v. California* (1967)—one observation for each year from 1967 through 2001. We then estimate separate logit models for positive and negative interpretation.[4] For both models, the standard errors accompanying the coefficient estimates are "robust" and allow residuals to be correlated across the multiple obser-

---

[2] Specifically, we include all orally argued full opinion and *per curiam* opinions (including judgments of the Court). These data are from Spaeth (1995, 2001). We exclude the 67 cases for which Spaeth did not assign an ideological direction to the case outcome.

[3] Some "Questioned" codes may not actually indicate that the Court negatively interpreted a precedent. We therefore read all treatment cases that Questioned a precedent and did not count treatments consisting of situations in which the Court indicated that Congress (or a past Court opinion) had previously overturned the precedent, but the treatment case did not actually negatively interpret the precedent.

[4] There are four alternative approaches we could employ here. First, we could estimate a single multinomial logit model instead of the two dichotomous logit models. The problem with this approach is that there is no clear way to handle situations in which a precedent is treated both negatively and positively in a given year. Nonetheless, to confirm our results, we estimated a multinomial logit model with a four-category dependent variable (positive interpretation, negative interpretation, both types of interpretation, and no interpretation) and the results were substantively the same as those produced by the logit models presented in table 4.1. This result is not surprising, since the multinomial logit is just a series of linked logit models. Second, we could estimate a bivariate probit model that allows for any correlation of residuals across the positive and negative interpretation models

vations associated with a given precedent (see White 1980). We also conducted diagnostics to check for any remaining autocorrelation, finding that it is not a problem.[5]

Independent Variables

IDEOLOGICAL DISTANCE

To measure the ideological distance between a precedent and the Court in each year, we rely upon data from Spaeth (1995, 2001). We measure the ideological orientation of a precedent as the percentage of the time the median member of the majority voting coalition in the precedent case voted liberally in the issue area of the case over his or her entire Court career.[6] To measure the ideological tenor of the Court in each year, we calculate the median value of the sitting justices' issue-specific liberalism scores (where we again use the percentage of the time each justice voted liberally over her career as a measure of individual policy preference). Our measure of *Ideological Distance* is the absolute value of

---

(Greene 1997). The only advantage to this approach is that it can be more efficient (i.e., the standard errors should be smaller). When estimating our models in such a manner, the substantive conclusions again remain the same as those revealed by our logit models. While, as expected, the standard errors are smaller in the bivariate probit model, the estimate for *Precedent Vitality* still remains statistically insignificant in the positive interpretation model. All other significance tests yield the same results as those presented here. Third, logit coefficient bias may be more problematic when the dependent variable is highly skewed. We therefore also ran our models using King and Zeng's (2001) rare events logit model. The results are highly consistent with the traditional logit results. Fourth, it might initially seem reasonable to estimate a two-stage model in which the first stage models whether a precedent is interpreted and the second stage models whether an interpreted precedent is interpreted positively or negatively. We rejected this approach because it does not permit a straightforward test of our theoretical model's predictions. We have theoretical predictions regarding the decision to treat a precedent positively. We also have hypotheses about the decision to treat a precedent negatively. However, our hypotheses are not easily converted to explaining positive treatment as opposed to negative treatment. For example, we expect the coefficient for the interaction term to be in the same direction in both our positive and negative interpretation models. In a two-stage model in which positive vs. negative treatment was the second stage, it is not at all clear what the expectation for the interaction term would be.

[5] First, we included a variable that captured the time since the Court's previous interpretation of a precedent (see Beck, Katz, and Tucker 1998), operationalized as length of time and the square of length of time, and our theoretical variables of interest manifest little change. Second, we included a one-year lag of the dependent variable as an independent variable, and our results are quite stable.

[6] The issue areas we refer to are those defined by Spaeth's (1995, 2001) 12 value areas: criminal procedure, civil rights, First Amendment, due process, privacy, attorneys, unions, economics, federal taxation, federalism, interstate relations, and judicial power. See Epstein et al. (1996, table 6.2) for this type of issue-specific voting records.

the difference between the issue-specific ideology of the median of the majority voting coalition in a precedent and the issue-specific ideology of the median member of the Court in the given year. We expect the coefficient for this variable to be negative for the positive treatment model and positive for the negative treatment model.

PRECEDENT VITALITY

To measure the vitality of a precedent, we use *Shepard's Citations* to count the number of times the Court's majority opinions interpreted the precedent in a positive or negative manner through the year prior to the one under consideration.[7] We then take the difference between the number of prior positive and negative interpretations. Positive values of this variable indicate that the Court has interpreted the precedent positively more often than negatively in years prior to the one under analysis. For example, if the precedent has been Followed three times and Distinguished once, *Precedent Vitality* will equal two. Negative scores indicate that the precedent has had more negative treatments than positive. We expect *Precedent Vitality* to have a negative coefficient in the negative treatment model. In the positive treatment model, our theory does not predict the sign for the *Precedent Vitality* coefficient.

Some might criticize our choice to measure legal vitality as a linear and cumulative function of prior interpretations. At this point, we think our approach is the most defensible one because it is the simplest and most straightforward, and no existing theory leads us to choose a more complex alternative. For example, we choose not to allow the effect of particular treatment of a precedent on that precedent's vitality to decay over

---

Like all proxies for theoretical constructs, our measure of *Ideological Distance* is imperfect. We realize that there may be instances in which, for example, a liberal majority voting coalition will establish a moderate or even somewhat conservative precedent. Nonetheless, we believe that our measure of *Ideological Distance* is reliable and valid. First, Epstein and Mershon (1996) show empirically that the approach we adopt is the best available way in which to measure the policy preferences of the justices. Scholars have therefore measured the policy preferences of justices using this approach in a variety of recent studies (e.g., Caldeira, Wright, and Zorn 1999; Maltzman, Spriggs, and Wahlbeck 2000; Spriggs and Hansford 2001). Second, Westerland (2003) shows that the median member of the majority coalition largely controls the policy content of the majority opinion. Therefore, the use of the median member's ideological position should be an appropriate proxy for the opinion's policy content.

[7] We exclude from this count any memorandum opinion that interpreted a precedent. We also exclude from the negative interpretation count any "Questioned" code that did not truly interpret the precedent. See chapter 3 for more details. If *Shepard's* codes a particular treatment opinion as negatively interpreting a precedent in more than one way (e.g., both Distinguished and Limited), we only count this as a single negative interpretation of the precedent. If a treatment opinion treats a precedent both positively and negatively, according to *Shepard's*, we include each of these treatments in their respective counts.

time (e.g., by counting it as less than one as the treatment ages). We do not want to assume that simply because a treatment of a precedent occurred some years ago, its influence goes down by some increment. In fact, as we pointed out in chapter 2, it is not clear whether older cases will be more vital or less vital. This idea also applies to younger and older treatments of a precedent. Simply because one treatment occurred some years before another treatment of a particular precedent does not necessarily mean that it is more relevant than the older one. In short, given the absence of a clear theoretical reason to do otherwise, we opt for the simplest way to measure vitality as a function of prior interpretations.

According to our argument, *Precedent Vitality* conditions the influence of *Ideological Distance*. We therefore include the interaction term *Ideological Distance × Precedent Vitality* in both of our models. Based on the above predictions, we expect this interaction term to have a positive coefficient in both the positive and negative treatment models. A positive estimate for the interaction term in the positive interpretation model would indicate that increases in precedent vitality decrease the negative effect of *Ideological Distance*. A positive estimate for the interaction term in the negative interpretation model would indicate that as the vitality of a precedent increases the positive effect of *Ideological Distance* grows in magnitude.

Control Variables

In addition to the three independent variables of theoretical interest, we also include a series of control variables that can be divided into two groups. These variables account for alternative explanations for our dependent variables and thus their inclusion increases our confidence in the estimates for our theoretical variables of interest. The first set is comprised of precedent characteristics that prior research suggests might influence *how* a precedent will be interpreted. Studies suggest that separate opinions and smaller decision coalitions will cause a precedent to be weaker and thus less likely to be interpreted positively and more likely to be interpreted negatively (e.g., Aldisert 1990, 632; Benesh and Reddick 2002; Danelski 1986; Johnson 1979, 1987; Pacelle and Baum 1992; Peczenik 1997). We therefore include control variables for the number of special concurring opinions accompanying a precedent (*Concurring Opinions in Precedent*) and the margin of votes by which the precedent was decided (*Voting Margin in Precedent*) in our empirical models.[8]

---

[8] We measure these variables, respectively, as the number of special concurring opinions accompanying the precedent and the number of justices in the majority decision coalition minus the number in the minority coalition. These data are from Spaeth (1995, 2001).

The second set of control variables contains factors that influence whether a precedent is likely to be interpreted by the Court. First, the extent to which a precedent is relevant, and thus might be interpreted by the Court, can be captured nicely by the total number of times the Court has legally interpreted the precedent in prior years (*Total Prior Interpretations*).[9] Second, a precedent dealing with an issue area that remains active on the Court's agenda (*Court Agenda*) is more likely to be interpreted.[10] Third, precedents dealing with a larger number and range of legal issues and legal provisions (*Breadth of Precedent*) may have a higher probability of being interpreted by the Court.[11] Fourth, cases based on constitutional interpretation (*Constitutional Precedent*) may be more likely to receive subsequent interpretation.[12] Fifth, any case that has previously been overruled by the Court (*Overruled Precedent*) is less likely to be legally interpreted.[13] We also include three variables that serve as proxies for the initial salience of a precedent: amici curiae participation in the precedent (*Amici Filings in Precedent*), media attention to the pre-

[9] Using *Shepard's Citations*, we count the total number of majority opinions that had interpreted a precedent—Followed, Explained, Harmonized, Distinguished, Criticized, Limited, Questioned, or Overruled—up to the year prior to the one being explained. We include the "neutral" treatment of precedent (Explained and Harmonized) in our count of the total number of interpretations because, while it does not represent substantive interpretation of precedent, it does nonetheless indicate that the case is still at risk of receiving such interpretation.

[10] To capture change in the Court's agenda over time, we first calculated the number of decisions handed down by the Court each year from 1946 through 2001 in each of Spaeth's (1995, 2001) 12 value areas. We then coded *Court Agenda* as the number of cases decided by the Court in the value area of the precedent for the given year.

[11] To measure this variable, we factor analyze two indicators of the breadth of a precedent: number of legal provisions and number of issues involved in the precedent case (Spaeth 1995, 2001). The former indicator refers to the specific legal provisions in the case, meaning the specific statute, treaty, or constitutional provisions being dealt with in the case. The latter pertains to the number of legal issues which are touched upon by the case. We then use the factor scores as our measure of *Precedent Breadth*.

[12] We code this variable as one if the Court decided the precedent based on constitutional grounds, using Spaeth (1995, 2001).

[13] We code this factor as one if the Court had previously overruled the precedent, using the coding protocols from Brenner and Spaeth (1995). We provide more detail on the coding of overruled precedents in chapter 5.

It is possible that congressional overrides of the Court's precedents involving statutory interpretation may affect whether the Court interprets such a precedent in the future. We therefore also estimated both of our logit models with an additional control variable equaling one if Congress had previously overridden the precedent and zero otherwise. The inclusion of this variable has no effect on the substantive results of the models, and its coefficient estimates are statistically insignificant. We used Eskridge (1991) for data on congressional overrides. Using his coding guidelines, we updated and backdated Eskridge's data so that we had the universe of congressional overrides of Court precedents decided between 1946 and 2001.

cedent when it was decided (*Media Coverage of Precedent*), and whether a precedent was decided by a full opinion, rather than per curiam (*Per Curiam Precedent*).[14] Finally, we control for the age of a precedent in year *y* by including a variable measured as the number of years since a precedent was decided and a variable for the square of this number (*Age of Precedent* and *Age of Precedent Squared*).[15]

RESULTS

Our aim in this chapter is to explain the occurrence and timing of the Court's interpretation of precedent. More specifically, we seek to explain whether, in a given year, the Court interprets a precedent positively or negatively. Before turning to a discussion of the results of our statistical models, we note that, as one would expect, the probability of any one precedent being interpreted in a particular year is low. For example, the average precedent has a 2.0% chance of being negatively interpreted by the Court in the average year and a 1.8% chance of being treated positively.[16] Yet, as we show below, the independent variables derived from our theory help to explain variation in the occurrence and timing of the treatment of precedent.

The Results of the Positive Interpretation Model

The results of our statistical models explaining how a precedent is interpreted in a given year are presented in table 4.1. The propositions developed in chapter 2 and the resulting hypotheses presented earlier in this chapter lead to two predictions regarding the direction of the coefficients for the variables included in the positive interpretation model. First, Hypothesis 4.1 states that increases in the distance between the Court's preferences and the policy set by a precedent will decrease the probability of

[14] We use the United States Supreme Court Data Base—Phase 2 (Gibson 1997) to calculate the number of amicus curiae briefs filed in each case. These data cover 1953–86, and we backdated and updated the data using the United States Reports. To account for the general increase in the number of briefs filed per case over this time period, we constructed a term-specific z-score, which indicates whether a given case had more (or less) filings than the average case heard during a term. *Media Coverage of Precedent* is coded as one if, on the day after the Court decided a case, it was mentioned as the lead case in a story on the front page of the *New York Times* (Epstein and Segal 2000). Using Epstein and Segal's coding protocol, we updated their data through 2001. We use Spaeth (1995, 2001) to determine whether a precedent was decided per curiam.

[15] Experimentation with the effect of precedent age on the likelihood of positive or negative interpretation suggests that the quadratic formulation is appropriate.

[16] These figures represent the average values of the two dependent variables.

TABLE 4.1
Logit Models of the Supreme Court's Interpretation of Precedent in a Given Year

Independent Variable	Positive Interpretation Coefficient (Robust S.E.)	Negative Interpretation Coefficient (Robust S.E.)
Ideological Distance (*ID*)	−.0067 (.0025)*	.0113 (.0019)*
Precedent Vitality (*V*)	.0134 (.0304)	−.1019 (.0262)*
Ideological Distance × Vitality (*ID* × *V*)	.0041 (.0018)*	.0042 (.0015)*
Control Variables:		
Concurring Opinions in Precedent	.1137 (.0335)	.0737 (.0323)*
Voting Margin in Precedent	−.0178 (.0076)	−.0190 (.0066)*
Total Prior Interpretations	.1817 (.0180)*	.1466 (.0149)*
Court Agenda	.0197 (.0021)*	.0153 (.0018)*
Breadth of Precedent	.1736 (.0469)*	.2068 (.0374)*
Amici Filings	.1130 (.0158)*	.0986 (.0141)*
Media Coverage	.2001 (.0567)*	.2729 (.0503)*
Per Curiam Precedent	−1.402 (.1673)*	−.8765 (.1260)*
Constitutional Precedent	.4104 (.0497)*	.5095 (.0421)*
Overruled Precedent	−.7135 (.3564)*	−.5535 (.2293)*
Age of Precedent	−.0944 (.0068)^	−.0750 (.0064)^
Age of Precedent Squared	.0006 (.0002)^	.0003 (.0002)
Constant	−3.541 (.0768)^	−3.677 (.0647)
Number of Observations	181,872	181,872
Log likelihood	−14418	−16108
Wald Test (Chi-square, 15 d.o.f.)	2083*	1832*

* $p \leq .05$ (one-tailed test, for directional hypotheses), ^ $p \leq .05$ (two-tailed test, for non-directional controls and constants).

the Court interpreting a precedent positively in a given year. This implies that the coefficient for *Ideological Distance* will be negative in direction. The estimate for this independent variable is, as we predict, negative and statistically significant. The coefficient indicates that when *Precedent Vitality* equals zero, the justices are indeed less likely to positively interpret precedents that they ideologically disfavor.

Second, Hypothesis 4.2 posits that increases in *Precedent Vitality* will attenuate the negative effect of *Ideological Distance*. The coefficient for *Ideological Distance* × *Precedent Vitality* is positive and statistically significant and thus provides initial support for this prediction. This result indicates that as *Precedent Vitality* increases, the negative effect of *Ideological Distance* diminishes. These two coefficients, taken together, show that the Court is more likely to positively interpret precedents it favors on policy grounds, but that this effect diminishes as a precedent has greater legal weight. The direction of the coefficient estimates for *Ideological Distance* and *Ideological Distance* × *Precedent Vitality* provide initial support for Hypotheses 4.1 and 4.2. But further assessment of these hypotheses and an examination of Hypothesis 4.3, which predicts that the justices will be more likely to positively interpret ideologically distant precedents that have greater vitality, require us to look at the conditional effects of these independent variables. That is, the inclusion of the interaction term in the model makes it necessary to look beyond the estimated coefficient for any one of these three variables.

Hypothesis 4.1 indicates that *Ideological Distance* will never exert a positive effect on the probability of positive interpretation, even when *Precedent Vitality* is at its maximum value. The full conditional coefficient for *Ideological Distance* can be expressed as: $-.0067 + (.0041 \times Precedent\ Vitality)$. This indicates that when *Precedent Vitality* is greater than or equal to 2 (2.2 standard deviations above its mean value), the effect of *Ideological Distance* shifts from negative to positive.[17] While this result does not perfectly comport with Hypothesis 4.1, the effect of *Ideological Distance* is negative for most of the range of *Precedent Vitality*. In fact, for all values of *Precedent Vitality* less than or equal to 0 the effect of *Ideological Distance* is negative and statistically significant.[18] Given the distribution of *Precedent Vitality*, this means that *Ideological Distance* has a statistically significant negative effect for 86.2% of the data. Thus, while these results could be somewhat cleaner, they are largely compatible with our argument that the Court is more likely to positively interpret precedents that it ideologically favors. For the vast majority of the observed range of *Precedent Vitality*, *Ideological Distance* has a statistically significant negative effect on the probability of a precedent being positively interpreted.

Hypothesis 4.2 posits that increases in *Precedent Vitality* will diminish the negative effect of *Ideological Distance*. As discussed in the preceding

---

[17] This positive effect, however, is not statistically distinguishable from zero for all but the most extreme positive values of *Precedent Vitality*. Specifically, *Ideological Distance* has a positive, significant effect when *Precedent Vitality* is greater than or equal to 12 (well under 0.1% of the data fall in this range).

[18] See Friedrich (1982) for a general explanation of how to calculate conditional standard errors when evaluating interaction terms, and Gill (n.d.) for a discussion of the interpretation of interaction terms in generalized linear models (such as the logit model). Throughout our empirical chapters we employ two-tailed significance tests ($p \leq .05$ level) when assessing the conditional effects of independent variables.

paragraphs, the logit model results indicate that *Precedent Vitality* exerts such a conditioning effect. While our theoretical model predicts that *Precedent Vitality* will not cause the effect of *Ideological Distance* to change directions, a sign change does occur at larger values of *Precedent Vitality*. Thus, the data provide strong, but somewhat qualified, support for Hypothesis 4.2.

Hypothesis 4.3 states that *Precedent Vitality* will exert a positive effect on the probability of positive interpretation if *Ideological Distance* is great. The full conditional coefficient for *Precedent Vitality*, as estimated in our logit model, can be represented as .0134 + (.0041 × *Ideological Distance*). Given that *Ideological Distance* is never negative, it should be clear from these coefficient estimates that the effect of this variable will, in fact, be positive for the entire range of *Ideological Distance*. The effect of *Precedent Vitality* is statistically significant for all values of *Ideological Distance* greater than 8.9.[19] This result indicates that *Precedent Vitality* not only exerts a statistically meaningful positive effect for precedents that are ideologically distant from the Court in year *y*, it also exerts a similar effect for precedents that are moderately close to the Court, ideologically speaking. This finding is fully compatible with Hypothesis 4.3.

In addition to largely confirming our theoretical predictions, these data yield an additional empirical result of some significance. While our theory leads to a prediction for the conditional effect of *Precedent Vitality* when *Ideological Distance* is large, we have no prediction regarding the direction of the coefficient for *Precedent Vitality*. Returning to our theoretical model, this coefficient depends on two competing considerations (represented in chapter 2 as $b_4 - b_3$) and we have no expectation regarding which of these two components is larger. We defined b_4 as the legitimization effect of precedent vitality, while b_3 is associated with the effect of precedent vitality on the extent to which the Court can alter current legal policy in a favorable manner.

Our results present an opportunity to test the relative effects of these two factors, since each offers a distinct prediction for ideologically favored precedents. If the legitimization component of the utility of positive interpretation is more important, then *Precedent Vitality* will have a positive coefficient and will thus have a positive effect on the probability of a precedent being interpreted positively as *Ideological Distance* approaches zero. If the influencing of extant precedent matters more, then *Precedent Vitality* will have a negative coefficient and thus a negative effect on the probability of an ideologically compatible precedent being interpreted positively.

According to the results of our logit model, the coefficient estimate for

---

[19] This value is .18 standard deviations below the mean value for *Ideological Distance*.

Precedent Vitality is positive, but it is not statistically distinguishable from zero.[20] As a result, we can tentatively conclude that b_3 is roughly similar in magnitude to b_4, although the positive direction of the coefficient implies that the latter effect might matter more. The benefit associated with legitimizing new legal policies is at least as important as the benefit associated with affecting the vitality of an existing precedent. This empirical result is important for our understanding of the interpretation of precedent because it suggests that while the justices make decisions based on their policy preferences, they are also constrained by the need to legitimize policy choices by relying on vital precedents. Moreover, these two factors work interdependently as the justices strive to both push existing precedent in directions they prefer and legitimize their current policy choices.

To further illustrate the nature of our results for the positive interpretation of precedent, figure 4.1 depicts the influence of *Ideological Distance* on the probability of a precedent being interpreted positively in a given year. Specifically, we present the predicted probabilities associated with the full range of values for *Ideological Distance* while *Precedent Vitality* is set at three distinct values. The curve represented by the solid line consists of the predicted probabilities of a precedent of average vitality being interpreted positively by the Court. The curves represented by the short dashes and long dashes consist of the predicted probabilities for a high vitality precedent (*Precedent Vitality* is set two standard deviations above its mean) and a low vitality precedent (*Precedent Vitality* is set two standard deviations below its mean), respectively.[21]

---

[20] Since we do not predict the sign on this coefficient, we use a two-tailed test of statistical significance ($p \leq .05$).

[21] All other independent variables are either set one standard deviation above their mean if they are positively signed or one standard deviation below their mean is they are negatively signed. Dichotomous independent variables are set at the value which increases the probability of interpretation. In short, the predicted probabilities in this figure and figure 4.2 are for precedents that have an above-average likelihood of being interpreted.

When generating predicted probabilities in an effort to illustrate an independent variable's effect, one should choose values for the other independent variables that reflect a realistic and interesting scenario. Researchers often, for example, set the other independent variables to their mean, median, or modal values, as they represent the most common scenario in the data. We chose to generate predicted probabilities for precedents with an above-average baseline probability of being interpreted for two reasons. First, the resulting predicted probabilities illustrate that while the probability of an "average" precedent being interpreted in a given year is very low, these probabilities do increase substantially when the independent variables move in the right direction. Second, we assume that the reader may be most interested in the effects of our independent variables in the set of precedents that actually have some meaningful probability of being interpreted. Of course, the general patterns (i.e., the direction of the relationships) in the predicted probabilities remain the same regardless of the values of the control variables. What changes are the size of the predicted probabilities and the steepness of the slopes.

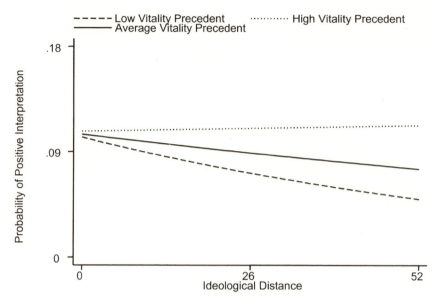

Figure 4.1. The effect of ideological distance and precedent vitality on the probability of a precedent being positively interpreted in a given year

Note: Ideological Distance is the absolute distance between the ideological position of the median member of the majority coalition in the precedent case and the median member of the Supreme Court in the given year. All other independent variables are set one standard deviation above their mean if they are positively signed or one standard deviation below their mean if they are negatively signed. Dichotomous independent variables are set at the value that increases the probability of interpretation. The predicted probabilities in this figure are thus for precedents that have an above-average likelihood of being interpreted.

This figure demonstrates that for precedents with a low amount of vitality, ideologically close Courts are much more likely to interpret the precedent positively than ideologically distant Courts. With a more vital precedent, however, ideologically close Courts have less incentive to positively interpret the precedent for purposes of influencing the state of the precedent. All Courts, however, have an increasing incentive to positively utilize (i.e., follow) a high vitality precedent for the purposes of legitimizing the new policy being established. As a result, the curves flatten out as *Precedent Vitality* increases. This figure therefore shows that the influence of *Ideological Distance* diminishes as *Precedent Vitality* increases.

In chapter 2, we laid out three different scenarios for the positive interpretation of precedent that were compatible with our theoretical predictions (see figure 2.1). Our empirical results, as demonstrated in figure 4.1, most closely resemble the second scenario depicted in figure 2.1. Again, this indicates that the incentives to alter existing precedent and to legitimize new policy choices are of approximately equal importance.

The Results of the Negative Interpretation Model

The hypotheses presented earlier in this chapter lead to three distinct predictions regarding the coefficients in our model explaining the likelihood of the Court interpreting a precedent negatively in a given year. All three predictions are supported by the results of this model estimation.[22] First, we expect increases in the ideological distance between the Court and a precedent to raise the probability of the precedent being treated negatively (Hypothesis 4.4). The coefficient estimate for *Ideological Distance* supports this hypothesis, as it is positive and statistically significant, indicating that when *Precedent Vitality* equals zero, the Court is more likely to negatively interpret precedents with which it disagrees. This result reveals that as the Court moves away from a precedent, ideologically speaking, the probability of that precedent being negatively interpreted goes up.

Our theoretical model further predicts that the coefficient for the interaction term will be positive in direction, since we expect increases in *Precedent Vitality* to amplify the positive effect of *Ideological Distance* (Hypothesis 4.5). The estimated coefficient for the interaction term supports this hypothesis, as it is both positive and statistically significant. This result indicates that as a precedent becomes more vital, the ideological distance between the Court and the precedent will exert a larger positive effect on the probability of the precedent being negatively treated. The importance of *Ideological Distance* increases with *Precedent Vitality*.

The estimate for *Precedent Vitality*, as predicted, is negative and statistically significant. This estimate reveals that when *Ideological Distance* is zero (i.e., the Court completely agrees with a precedent), the probability

---

[22] In order to assess whether the results of the negative interpretation model are being driven by the stronger forms of negative interpretation (e.g., interpretations that Limit or Criticize a precedent), we also estimated the model including only weak negative interpretations (i.e., interpretations that Distinguish a precedent) in the dependent variable. The results for this model are similar to the results obtained when all forms of negative interpretation are included together. Furthermore, the results, as seen in chapter 5, are also quite similar when looking at the strongest form of negative interpretation (the overruling of precedent). The results are also largely comparable if one uses a dependent variable representing "strong" negative interpretation (*Shepard's* codes for Overruled, Limited, Criticized, and Questioned). Therefore, it appears that the results presented here are not being driven by any one type of negative interpretation.

of negative treatment decreases as *Precedent Vitality* increases (see Hypothesis 4.6). While the Court is less likely to negatively interpret ideologically favored precedents, this tendency is even more pronounced when those precedents are particularly vital. As indicated by the utility function in chapter 2, this empirical relationship results from both the justices' need to legitimize their new policy choices and their desire to make existing policy more consistent with their preferences.

To assess fully the fit of the data with our hypotheses, we must move beyond the estimated coefficient of each independent variable and consider conditional effects. That is, our theory predicts that the effect of *Ideological Distance* will differ based on the level of *Precedent Vitality*. The conditional effect of *Ideological Distance* on the probability of the Court treating a precedent negatively in year y is captured by the conditional coefficient .0113 + (.0042 × *Precedent Vitality*). This effect is positive and statistically significant for all values of *Precedent Vitality* greater than or equal to −1 (which is approximately one standard deviation below the mean value of *Precedent Vitality*).[23] Thus, the results for *Ideological Distance* largely support Hypothesis 4.4, as there is a positive and significant effect for 94.4% of the data. The data also confirm Hypothesis 4.5, which predicts that the effect of the ideological distance between the Court and a precedent will be more pronounced for precedents that are more legally vital.

Hypothesis 4.6 posits that *Precedent Vitality* will negatively influence the likelihood of a precedent being interpreted negatively if the Court in year y is ideologically close to the precedent. Based on our logit model results, the conditional coefficient for *Precedent Vitality* is −.1019 + (.0042 × *Ideological Distance*). When *Ideological Distance* is less than 14.7 (0.37 standard deviations above the mean), *Precedent Vitality* exerts a negative and statistically significant effect. This result clearly comports with Hypothesis 4.6. While we make no prediction about the effect of *Precedent Vitality* when *Ideological Distance* is large, our results indicate that the effect of *Precedent Vitality* is statistically indistinguishable from zero for large values of *Ideological Distance*, although this effect does become positive in direction when *Ideological Distance* is greater than 24.2.

In figure 4.2, we graph the probability of negative interpretation as a function of both *Ideological Distance* and *Precedent Vitality*. The curve consisting of a solid line depicts the predicted probabilities of a precedent of average vitality being interpreted negatively by the Court. The

---

[23] The full effect of *Ideological Distance* actually becomes negative when *Precedent Vitality* is less than or equal to −3. Even for the lowest value of *Precedent Vitality*, this negative effect is not statistically distinguishable from zero.

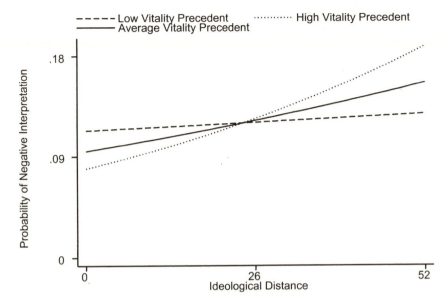

Figure 4.2. The effect of ideological distance and precedent vitality on the probability of a precedent being negatively interpreted in a given year

Note: Ideological Distance is the absolute distance between the ideological position of the median member of the majority coalition in the precedent case and the median member of the Supreme Court in the given year. All other independent variables are set one standard deviation above their mean if they are positively signed or one standard deviation below their mean if they are negatively signed. Dichotomous independent variables are set at the value that increases the probability of interpretation. The predicted probabilities in this figure are thus for precedents that have an above-average likelihood of being interpreted.

curves represented by the short dashes and long dashes represent the predicted probabilities for a high vitality precedent (*Precedent Vitality* is set two standard deviations above its mean) and a low vitality precedent (*Precedent Vitality* is set two standard deviations below its mean), respectively.

This figure further illustrates the fit between our theory and the data. Negative interpretation is not just a function of *Ideological Distance* or *Precedent Vitality*; it is a function of the interaction between these two variables. Specifically, the effect of *Ideological Distance* is conditioned by the vitality of the precedent. Likewise, the influence of *Precedent Vitality* is contingent on the compatibility between the Court's policy preferences and the precedent. The data reveal that the Court will be most likely to interpret a precedent negatively if the precedent is both ideologically distant from the Court and highly vital. Conversely, the Court will be least likely to treat a precedent negatively if the precedent is ideologically close and vital. In short, *Precedent Vitality* acts to amplify the effect of *Ideological Distance*.

These results also give us leverage on the relative importance of the two aspects of the effect of *Precedent Vitality* on the negative interpretation of precedent. While we have a hypothesis for the conditional effect of *Precedent Vitality* for low values of *Ideological Distance*, we have no hypothesis for its effect when *Ideological Distance* is high. Figure 4.2 reveals that *Precedent Vitality* has a positive influence on the probability of negative interpretation when the precedent is ideologically distant from the Court. The more vital an ideologically distant precedent, the more likely it is to be treated negatively by the Court in a given year. This effect suggests that when it comes to the negative interpretation of precedent, the desire to affect extant precedent may be more important to the justices than concerns about the legitimacy of new policy choices. We emphasize that these data are only suggestive, because this effect is not statistically significant (using a two-tailed test). Thus, while the empirical relationships evident in figure 4.2 appear most consistent with the first theoretical scenario depicted in figure 2.2, we cannot rule out the possibility that the data might actually be consistent with the second scenario. We can, however, conclusively say that the data do not comport with the third theoretical scenario, meaning that the legitimacy aspect of vitality is not dominant.

The Control Variables

We now turn to a brief discussion of the results for the control variables in the two logit models. Two of these variables are included because prior research suggests they may affect the type of interpretation given a precedent. These variables perform as expected in the negative interpretation model but not in the positive interpretation model. The number of special concurring opinions accompanying the precedent increases the probability of negative interpretation but does not decrease the likelihood of the precedent being treated positively. Similarly, larger voting margins in a precedent case decrease the probability of negative interpretation but do not increase the likelihood of positive treatment. The fact that the coefficients for these variables are actually in the same direction across the two models suggests that they affect the probability of interpretation, not the type of interpretation. In other words, precedents set by relatively small majorities appear more likely to be interpreted either positively or negatively, perhaps because they tend to deal with particularly controversial legal questions. This is an interesting result because it demonstrates that a common contention in the literature (e.g., Johnson 1987; Klein 2002; Pacelle and Baum 1992; Spriggs and Hansford 2001) does not comport with reality.

We also include a set of control variables that might affect the likelihood of the Supreme Court interpreting a precedent, either positively or negatively. The positive and statistically significant estimates for *Total Prior Interpretations* demonstrate that the Court is more likely to interpret precedents (either positively or negatively) that have been interpreted in the past. The prevalence of the precedent's central legal issue in the Court's agenda in a given year also exerts a positive effect on the likelihood of being interpreted in that year. Further, these statistical models suggest that the Court is more likely to interpret precedents that are broad, constitutional, received media or organized interest attention, were decided by full opinion rather than per curiam, and have not been overruled.

The variables controlling for the age of a precedent indicate that, all else being equal, age initially decreases the probability of a precedent being interpreted. As age increases, however, the negative effect of age diminishes.[24] To some extent, this result supports the argument made by others that the informational value of a precedent may decrease over time (see Kosma 1998; Landes and Posner 1976), although it does not decrease at a constant rate.

Explaining the Negative Interpretation of Anders

Finally, let us return to the substantive example of negative interpretation with which we introduced the chapter and place this example in the context of our model. Why did the Rehnquist Court negatively interpret *Anders v. California* (1967) in 2000? To start, the contemporary Rehnquist Court has been quite conservative in the issue area of criminal procedure, while the justices in the majority in *Anders* were considerably more liberal.[25] Thus, the *Anders* precedent was negatively treated by a Court that was ideologically distant from the policy set by *Anders*. The results from our quantitative analysis of the negative interpretation

---

[24] The estimated coefficients for *Age of Precedent* and *Age of Precedent Squared* indicate, for example, that the probability of a precedent being positively interpreted will decrease as the precedent ages, until the precedent is 79 years old. At that point, the effect of precedent age flattens out and then becomes positive. We would not make much of this change in the direction of the effect, however, given that it occurs well outside the range of values found in the data for this variable.

[25] The *Ideological Distance* between the *Anders* precedent and the 2000 Court was 38.5 (2.6 standard deviations above the mean), as the Court median in 2000 in the issue area of criminal procedure was a somewhat conservative 44.7 and the precedent's ideological placement was a much more liberal 83.2.

indicate that the sizable ideological distance between *Anders* and the Court of 2000 contributed to the negative treatment that this precedent received.

The treatment of *Anders* also helps to illustrate the interactive effect of *Precedent Vitality* and *Ideological Distance*. Prior to 2000, *Anders* had been positively interpreted (Followed) by the Court on three occasions.[26] As indicated by our quantitative results, ideologically distant precedents are particularly vulnerable if they are relatively vital. In short, our results suggest that *Anders* is very much the sort of precedent that the Rehnquist Court of 2000 would have liked to treat in a negative manner. Not surprisingly, the Court interpreted *Anders*, a case with an above-average amount of vitality that it ideologically disapproved of, negatively in a way that would likely lead to outcomes more in keeping with its policy preferences.

CONCLUSION

At the center of our theoretical argument is the notion that justices interpret precedent in order to impact distributional outcomes. By interpreting precedent, they can influence the scope and vitality of prior legal rules, as well as justify new policies being set. Thus, we argue that precedents will be interpreted based on the ideological distance between the Court and the precedent, the vitality of the precedent, and, importantly, the interaction between these variables.

In this chapter, we tested this theoretical conception by examining the Court's interpretation of a large set of precedents over time. We specifically looked at the interpretations that Supreme Court precedents decided between the 1946 and 1999 terms received by the end of 2001. Despite the broad focus of this analysis, our empirical results provide considerable support for our theoretical argument. First, we demonstrate that the Court's interpretation of precedent depends on the extent to which the justices agree with a precedent. As the ideological distance between the Court and a precedent increases, the likelihood of the Court interpreting the precedent positively decreases, while the likelihood of the Court interpreting it negatively increases.

Second, we demonstrate that the vitality of a precedent influences the Court's decision about how to interpret it. More specifically, we find that precedent vitality conditions the effect of ideological distance on the

---

[26] *Anders* had also been interpreted negatively (Distinguished) once, yielding a *Precedent Vitality* of two (2.1 standard deviations above the mean) for the year 2000. Not included in this count are five summary dispositions in which the Court relied on *Anders*.

Court's decision to positively or negatively interpret a precedent. Precedent vitality diminishes the negative effect of ideological distance on the probability of positive interpretation and accentuates the positive effect of ideological distance on the likelihood of negative treatment. For example, the justices are more likely to negatively treat a precedent they dislike on ideological grounds if that precedent is currently quite vital.

We also found tentative evidence that when it comes to the positive interpretation of precedent, the potentially competing goals of maximizing the legitimacy of new precedent and influencing the state of existing policy appear to be of roughly equal importance to the justices. Regarding the negative interpretation of precedent, the Court seems to be somewhat more motivated by the desire to shape existing precedent than by concerns about the need to legitimize new policy choices. This is a point we will return to in the concluding chapter.

It is worth reiterating that these results confirm our argument that the role of *stare decisis* at the Court (at least as applied to the interpretation of precedent) is not simply that of a constraint on judicial choices. Rather, as we argued in chapter 2, precedent offers the Court both an opportunity to shape legal policy and a constraint in terms of the need to legitimize policy choices with precedents that possess greater legal vitality. Our empirical analyses demonstrate that the legal vitality of precedent does indeed play these two, somewhat competing, roles. This is especially the case for the positive interpretation of precedent.

On a related note, our results indicate that the vitality of a precedent exerts an independent, albeit conditional, causal effect on how the Court interprets the precedent. We emphasize this point because previous studies of precedent have had difficulty controlling for the potential endogeneity of precedent (e.g., Richards and Kritzer 2002; Spriggs and Hansford 2001; Wahlbeck 1997). This difficulty results because the basic premise of the norm of precedent is that prior actions on the part of the Court will constrain its future behavior. Thus, one must be able to demonstrate that the Court's prior behavior is causally related to its present behavior and is not the effect of unobserved and unmeasured forces influencing legal treatment at both points in time (meaning any observed effect is spurious).

If we simply demonstrated that precedent vitality exerted an additive effect on the interpretation of precedent, then it would be difficult to disentangle whether precedent vitality was causing the interpretation of precedent or whether it was a proxy for the Court's continuing support for a precedent. This support could result either from an ideological effect not captured by our model (perhaps as a result of error in our measurement of the ideological distance between the Court and a precedent) or from some propensity on the Court's part to always support "high" quality precedents over "low" quality precedents (where quality could be thought of as a static element of the precedent).[27] That is, if we only demonstrated that past negative interpretations preceded subsequent negative interpretations, a skeptic might suggest that the Court simply did not like the precedent and thus treated it negatively in the past as well as at the point in time under consideration. In this situation, the argument could be made that the relationship between the vitality of the precedent and the treatment of the precedent at any given point in time is spurious. The real driving factor could be the Court's continuing dislike of the precedent, for ideological or nonideological reasons.

Our theory and thus our statistical models are not particularly susceptible to this problem. As a result, we are confident that our empirical results regarding precedent vitality cannot be simply explained as a function of the Court's dislike of a precedent. First, and most importantly, our theoretical model predicts a nonadditive relationship between precedent vitality and the interpretation of precedent; and this prediction is at odds with the claim that the effect of vitality might be spurious. For example, we predict that an increase in *Precedent Vitality* will magnify the positive effect of *Ideological Distance* on the probability of negative interpretation. If our measure of vitality actually captured some static notion of precedent quality or any unmeasured ideological distance between the Court and the precedent, then it is hard to conceive of a reason why *Precedent Vitality* would act to condition the effect *of Ideological Distance* in such a manner. Rather, under this latter conception, *Precedent Vitality* should be negatively related to the negative interpretation of precedent, but it should not act to condition the effect of *Ideological Distance*. In short, if our measure of vitality simply captured residual ideological distance or the quality of the precedent, then there is no reason why the effect of *Ideological Distance* would be conditional based on *Precedent Vitality*.

Our data provide additional evidence to demonstrate that the effect of vitality is not spurious. We show, for example, that the Court is most likely to negatively interpret a precedent that is both ideologically distant from the Court and particularly vital (i.e., has been treated positively in the past). This result suggests that the effect of precedent vitality

[27] Given the way we measure *Precedent Vitality*, it is not serving as a surrogate for the relevance of a precedent at time t. Our measure cannot act as a surrogate for relevance because both large positive and large negative values indicate that the precedent has been treated a greater number of times in the past. For prior interpretations to act as a surrogate for relevance, it would be preferable to simply include a total count of prior interpretations (where only larger positive values indicate a greater number of prior interpretations). That is precisely why we include a control variable, *Total Prior Interpretations*, which is measured as the total number of times a precedent has been treated by the Court in the past.

cannot simply be chalked up to an insufficient accounting for the effect of the ideological distance between the precedent and the subsequent Court. The view of vitality as spurious would predict just the opposite effect (i.e., the Court would be more likely to negatively interpret a precedent that has been treated negatively in the past and thus has a low level of vitality). For these reasons, we conclude that the vitality of a precedent does play a meaningful role in how the Court interprets it.

We close by highlighting that the most critical test of our theoretical argument involves the interaction term, *Ideological Distance* × *Vitality*. Neither of the prevailing conceptions of Court decision making, the legal and attitudinal models, would predict such an effect. Attitudinalists would argue that judicial ideology is the key variable, and thus *Ideological Distance* would motivate the treatment of precedent. Legalists, by contrast, would argue that precedent matters most, and thus *Precedent Vitality* would act as a constraint. Neither, however, would predict the conditional relationship between these two variables that is evident in our model and data. Simply put, judicial ideology and precedent vitality do not work in isolation from one another; they operate in concert to produce legal change.

CHAPTER FIVE

The Overruling of Precedent

SEARCH WARRANTS can only be issued if the police officer seeking the warrant can demonstrate probable cause. Often, it is necessary to rely on information provided by an informant when attempting to meet the probable cause requirement. In *Aguilar v. Texas* (1964), the Supreme Court established a two-pronged test for determining whether informant-provided information can constitute the probable cause needed for a magistrate to issue a search warrant. To satisfy the first prong, the police officer requesting the warrant must indicate the basis of the knowledge claimed by the informant. To satisfy the second prong, the officer must demonstrate either the reliability of the informant or the credibility of the information. Five years later, this two-pronged test was refined and reinforced in *Spinelli v. United States* (1969). Presumably, this pair of precedents influenced the behavior of police officers seeking search warrants and the magistrates charged with issuing such warrants by making it considerably more difficult to rely on informant-provided information when establishing probable cause.

Nearly two decades after the *Aguilar* decision, the Supreme Court chose to do away with this two-pronged test. The Court, in *Illinois v. Gates* (1983), formally rejected the *Aguilar* and *Spinelli* precedents and replaced the relatively rigid two-pronged test with a more flexible "totality-of-the-circumstances" test. This new test presented a substantially lower hurdle for police officers attempting to use informant testimony to obtain a search warrant. Simply put, the overruling of *Aguilar* and *Spinelli* was good news for police officers and bad news for criminal suspects.

The norm of *stare decisis* is central to our legal system, and adherence to precedent yields a variety of benefits, including clarity, stability, and predictability in the law (Douglas [1949] 1979; Powell 1990; Stevens 1983), efficiency (Landes and Posner 1976; Stevens 1983), judicial legitimacy (Knight and Epstein 1996), and fairness (Freed 1996; Padden 1994). Both justices and legal scholars agree that, for these reasons, the Supreme Court should be reluctant to overrule one of its precedents. Nonetheless, precedents such as *Aguilar* and *Spinelli* have been overruled by the Court. In fact, Brenner and Spaeth (1995) document that the Court overrules an average of approximately three of its precedents per term.[1] By overruling one of its precedents, the Court clearly signals an end to the applicability of the legal rule established by the precedent and replaces the old legal rule with one that is fundamentally different in nature.

This book is about one aspect of legal change—the interpretation of precedent at the Supreme Court. The overruling of a Court precedent is clearly the most extreme type of precedent interpretation available to the justices and represents a dramatic form of legal change. In this chapter, we temporarily narrow our analysis and focus on this one type of interpretation. We attempt to answer the question, when and why will the Supreme Court overrule one of its precedents? Why are precedents like *Aguilar* and *Spinelli* overruled, while other precedents continue to endure? We apply our theoretical framework to this question and test three primary hypotheses with our data on the Court's treatment of precedents established from the 1946 to 1999 terms. Using these data, we develop a duration model explaining the "survival" of Court precedent over time.

Hypotheses

Given the political and legal importance of the overruling of precedent, researchers have focused more on this type of treatment of precedent than other, less severe forms of precedent interpretation. Prior research suggests that the overruling of precedent results from the ideological leanings of the justices (e.g., Banks 1992; Brenner and Spaeth 1995; Ulmer 1959), the legal basis of the precedent (Banks 1992), and the size of the majority coalition and presence of separate opinions in the precedent-setting case (Banks 1992; Brenner and Spaeth 1995; Schmidhauser 1962; Ulmer 1959). We contend that the theoretical framework presented in chapter 2 will apply to the decision to overrule a precedent, just as it applies to other, milder forms of the interpretation of precedent.

In chapter 2, we argue that the justices' motivation to interpret precedent derives from both the desire to impact the current state of legal policy and the need to legitimize new policy choices. The former incentive leads the justices to treat precedent based on its compatibility with their policy preferences and the vitality of the precedent, which we conceptualize as the legal authority of a precedent as seen in the Court's prior interpretation of it. The latter incentive encourages justices to treat precedent solely based on its legal vitality. The Court's interpretation of precedent thus depends on the interaction between the justices' policy goals and the legal vitality of a precedent.

[1] Brenner and Spaeth coded all the instances in which the Supreme Court overruled one of its precedents during the time span of 1946 to 1992.

Our three propositions about the Court's decision to interpret a precedent negatively lead to three specific hypotheses about the overruling of precedent, which are functionally identical to the three hypotheses regarding negative interpretation in the preceding chapter.

> *Hypothesis 5.1:* *The greater the ideological distance between a precedent and the Court in year y, the greater the probability that the Court will overrule the precedent in year y (see Proposition 2.4).*

> *Hypothesis 5.2:* *The more vital a precedent is in year y, the larger the positive effect of ideological distance on the probability of a precedent being overruled in year y (see Proposition 2.5).*

> *Hypothesis 5.3:* *The vitality of a precedent in year y will exert a negative effect on the probability of the precedent being overruled in year y, if the precedent is ideologically close to the Court (see Proposition 2.6).*

DATA AND MEASUREMENT

Dependent Variable

The observed dependent variable in our analysis here is whether the Supreme Court overruled a given precedent in a given year. We use in this chapter the same 6,363 Supreme Court precedents discussed in chapter 3 and analyzed in chapter 4. To determine whether and when each of these precedents was subsequently overruled by the Supreme Court, we relied primarily on Brenner and Spaeth's (1995) list of overruled cases from 1946 to 1992.[2] We updated this list by applying Bren-

---

[2] We chose not to rely solely on *Shepard's* when determining whether a precedent has been overruled because, for our purposes here, Brenner and Spaeth's (1995) data are more suitable. As we noted in chapter 3, *Shepard's* coding of positive and negative interpretations of Supreme Court precedent is highly reliable, but can be somewhat underinclusive. This underinclusiveness occurs because *Shepard's* only assigns the Overruling code if there is specific language in the opinion stating that the precedent is overruled. Brenner and Spaeth's coding rules are more flexible and allow, for instance, for a precedent to be listed as being overruled if a dissenting opinion in the overruling case indicates as much or if a subsequent Court opinion indicates that a previous Court opinion overruled a precedent. If we use *Shepard's* coding of overruled precedents, however, we obtain approximately the same results as are generated with the Brenner and Spaeth data. Specifically, the coefficients (standard errors) for our theoretical variables of interest are: *Ideological Distance*, .055 (.011); *Precedent Vitality*, −.693 (.185); *Ideological Distance × Vitality*, .016 (.005). The only difference in the control variables across the two dependent variables is that when

ner and Spaeth's coding rules to precedents coded as overruled in Spaeth (2001), the Congressional Research Service's *The Constitution of the United States of America, Analysis and Interpretation*, and *Shepard's Citations*. This approach yields a total of 107 cases that the Supreme Court both decided and then overruled between 1946 and 2001.

For the 107 overruled precedents, the average length of "survival" is 15.2 years. That is, the average overruled precedent in our data was overruled approximately 15 years after it had been established by the Court. For cases that are overruled, the minimum length of survival in our data is less than one year, while the maximum survival time is 41 years.[3]

With these data, we created a dataset containing an observation for each precedent in each year of its existence, including the year it was decided and every subsequent year until the case was overruled or until the year 2001.[4] The observed dependent variable is whether the precedent in question was overruled in the given year.

To test our hypotheses regarding the overruling of precedent, we estimate a Cox proportional hazards model. The Cox model is a member of the duration model family.[5] The observed dependent variable in a duration model is whether the event occurred during a particular point in time, or, put differently, the length of time before the event in question occurs. The unobserved dependent variable is the hazard rate, or instantaneous risk that the event will occur at time t, conditional on the event not having occurred previously. A hazard rate is essentially analogous to a probability, except that a hazard rate does not have an upper bound of one. For the purposes of our analysis, the hazard rate is the risk that a precedent will be overruled by the Court in a particular year, given that it has not been previously overruled.

---

using *Shepard's* data on overrules, the estimate for *Amici Filings* is not statistically significant. The fact that we get such similar results with both measures of our dependent variable increases our confidence in the model and in both measures of the overruling of precedent.

[3] In our data, a duration of one year represents a precedent that was overruled in the same year that it was decided. This occurred once during the time span of our study, with *Yates v. Evatt* (1991) being overruled by *Estelle v. McGuire* (1991). *Aero Mayflower Transit Co. v. Board of Railroad Commissioners* (1947) and *United States v. Bramblett* (1955) are the two precedents with the longest length of time between being decided and overruled by the Court (40 years). They were respectively overruled by *American Trucking Assns., Inc. v. Scheiner* (1987) and *Hubbard v. United States* (1995).

[4] The number of observations utilized in the analysis in this chapter is somewhat smaller than the number in the previous chapter because here we do not include observations occurring after a precedent has been overruled.

[5] Duration models are also referred to as survival or event history models. For a discussion of duration models and their application in political science, see Box-Steffensmeier and Jones (2004).

We employ a duration model here because this type of model is specifically designed for the type of data we are analyzing in this chapter. Duration models allow researchers to estimate the effect of independent variables on both the hazard of an event occurring in a given time period and the length of time that a case "survives" before the event occurs. Further, duration models can handle the inevitable right-censoring associated with studying the overruling of precedent. Previously, researchers have had to choose between either examining only the precedents that have been overruled or making the untenable assumption that all precedents that have yet to be overruled will not be overruled in the future.

From the family of duration models, we choose the Cox proportional hazards model because it makes no assumptions regarding the nature of the baseline hazard rate (i.e., the underlying hazard for each time t, once all the independent variables are controlled for). We estimate this model with "robust" standard errors, which allow errors to be correlated across the multiple observations associated with a precedent (see White 1980).

Independent Variables

The three key independent variables in this model are the same as those in chapter 4. *Ideological Distance* is included and is again measured as the absolute value of the difference between the issue-specific ideology of the median of the majority voting coalition for the precedent and the issue-specific ideology of the median member of the Court in the given year. The coefficient for this variable should be positive in direction. *Precedent Vitality* is the difference between the number of prior positive and negative Court interpretations of the precedent. We expect the coefficient for this variable to be negative. We also include the interaction term *Ideological Distance × Precedent Vitality* and predict that it will have a positive coefficient, indicating that as the vitality of a precedent increases, the positive effect of *Ideological Distance* on the hazard of a precedent being overruled grows in magnitude.

In addition to our three independent variables of theoretical interest, we also include virtually the same set of control variables utilized in chapter 4. Specifically, we include *Concurring Opinions in Precedent, Voting Margin in Precedent, Total Prior Interpretations, Court Agenda, Breadth of Precedent, Constitutional Precedent, Amici Filings in Precedent, Media Coverage of Precedent,* and *Per Curiam Precedent* as control variables. Detailed descriptions of the measurement of all of these variables can be found in chapter 4. There are three control variables in the chapter 4 models that are not included in the Cox model of the overruling of

Table 5.1
Cox Regression Model of the Overruling of Supreme Court Precedent

Independent Variable	Estimated Coefficient	Robust Standard Error
Ideological Distance (ID)	.0394*	.0093
Precedent Vitality (V)	−.3901*	.1505
Ideological Distance × Vitality (ID × V)	.0092*	.0047
Control Variables:		
Concurring Opinions in Precedent	.2276	.1892
Voting Margin in Precedent	−.1643*	.0358
Total Prior Interpretations	.0836*	.0276
Court Agenda	.0165*	.0095
Breadth of Precedent	.3968*	.1506
Amici Filings	.1170*	.0640
Media Coverage	−.0694	.2542
Per Curiam Precedent	−.2794	.5265
Constitutional Precedent	.5571*	.2206
Number of Cases	6,363	
Total Time at Risk (Years)	179,653	
Log-likelihood	−837	
Wald Test (Chi-square, 15 d.o.f.)	142*	

*$p \leq .05$ (one-tailed test).

precedent. We do not include *Overruled Precedent* because we exclude observations occurring after a precedent has been overruled. We do not include *Age of Precedent* and *Age of Precedent Squared* because the Cox model already allows the baseline hazard of a precedent being overruled to vary by age.[6] In other words, the Cox model controls for any effect that precedent age might have on the likelihood of a precedent being overruled.

Results

The results of our Cox proportional hazards model estimation are displayed in table 5.1. A Wald test yields a statistically significant chi-squared statistic, indicating that the inclusion of the independent variables leads to a better model fit than a baseline hazard–only model. The Cox model

[6] Cox models allow time to have a non-parametric effect on the hazard rate.

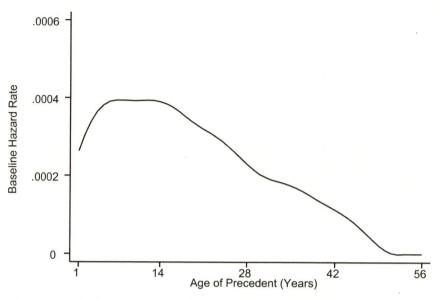

Figure 5.1. The baseline hazard of a precedent being overruled in a given year of its "life"

Note: The baseline hazard estimates have been lowess smoothed.

makes no assumptions about the shape or form of the baseline hazard, but it is possible to retrieve estimates of the baseline hazard of a precedent being overruled at various points in time. Figure 5.1 contains a graphical depiction of the baseline hazard estimates. To better display the underlying trends in the baseline hazard, we smoothed it using the lowess approach. The smoothed estimates reveal that the baseline hazard of a precedent being overruled increases for the first few years of a precedent's existence. The baseline hazard then flattens and ultimately decreases as the precedent ages. The conclusion we can draw from this result is that, controlling for the effect of all the independent variables included in the model, precedent age initially exerts a positive effect on the likelihood of a precedent being overruled. As the precedent gets older, however, the effect of age eventually becomes negative and the likelihood of the precedent being overruled begins to decrease. Old precedents (50 + years old) are very unlikely to be overruled, according to these estimates of the baseline hazard.

Before discussing the coefficient estimates for the independent variables in the Cox model, it is important to note that in a duration model the coefficients represent the effect of the independent variable on the hazard of the event occurring in year y. As the hazard of a precedent being overruled increases, the expected duration or lifespan of the precedent decreases. Thus, if an independent variable has a positive effect on the hazard rate, then it has a negative effect on the duration of the precedent's lifespan.

Returning to table 5.1, the coefficient estimates for the three central variables provide initial support for our three hypotheses regarding the overruling of precedent. The positive and statistically significant estimate for *Ideological Distance* indicates that, when *Precedent Vitality* equals zero, the less the Court likes a precedent, from a policy perspective, the more inclined the Court is to overrule the precedent. This result supports Hypothesis 5.1.

We also expect that the coefficient for the interaction term will be positive. As *Precedent Vitality* increases, the positive effect of *Ideological Distance* on the hazard of a precedent being overruled should be amplified (Hypothesis 5.2). The estimate for the interaction term conforms with this expectation, as it is positive in direction and statistically significant. The more vital a precedent is, the greater the effect that ideological distance has on the hazard of the precedent being overruled. This particular result also shows one reason why precedent vitality is important at the Court. The justices recognize that lower court judges and other actors are more likely to follow and implement precedents with greater vitality. As a result, they are most inclined to overrule precedents that are both ideologically distant from their preferred policy and legally vital.

The estimate for *Precedent Vitality*, as predicted, is negative and significant. This estimate indicates that when *Ideological Distance* is zero (i.e., a precedent is fully compatible with the preferences of the median member of the Court), the hazard of a precedent being overruled decreases as *Precedent Vitality* increases (see Hypothesis 5.3). This effect is a result of a combination of the desire to influence existing precedent (i.e., b_7 in the model presented in chapter 2) and to legitimize the new legal policy being established (i.e., b_8).

The direction of the coefficient estimates provides initial support for our hypotheses, but we need to consider the conditional effects of these variables, just as we did in the previous chapter. Hypotheses 5.1 and 5.2 imply that *Ideological Distance* will always have a positive net effect on the hazard of a precedent being overruled. No value of *Precedent Vitality* should lead to *Ideological Distance* having a negative effect. An examination of the conditional coefficient for *Ideological Distance* (i.e., including the coefficient for the individual variable and the coefficient associated with the interaction term) reveals that this variable exerts a statistically significant positive effect for all values of *Precedent Vitality* greater than −2 (2.0 standard deviations below the mean value).[7] Thus, *Ideological Distance* exhibits the hypothesized effect in a statistically significant sense for approximately 95% of the data (i.e., the percentage of the observations in which *Precedent Vitality* is greater than −2).

Hypothesis 5.3 indicates that for precedents that are ideologically close to the Court in year *y*, the vitality of the precedent will have a negative effect on the hazard of a precedent being overruled in year *y*. The conditional coefficient for *Precedent Vitality*, according to the estimates of our Cox model, is −.3901 + (.0092 × *Ideological Distance*). Based on this conditional coefficient and the accompanying conditional standard error, we can conclude that *Precedent Vitality* exerts a negative and statistically significant effect when *Ideological Distance* is less than 27.4 (1.6 standard deviations above the mean value). This result fully supports Hypothesis 5.3. Our theoretical model makes no prediction regarding the conditional effect of *Precedent Vitality* when the Court is ideologically distant from a precedent. Our results indicate that this variable exerts a positive effect on the hazard of a precedent being overruled if the precedent is ideologically incompatible with the Court, although this particular effect is not statistically significant.

The conditional effects of *Ideological Distance* and *Precedent Vitality* on the hazard of a precedent being overruled are illustrated in figure 5.2.[8] As this figure reveals, for low (two standard deviations below the mean), average, and high (two standard deviations above the mean) levels of *Precedent Vitality*, increases in *Ideological Distance* lead to an increase in the risk of a precedent being overruled (as predicted by Hypothesis 5.1). The predicted hazards also indicate that low vitality precedents are at greater risk of being overruled if *Ideological Distance* is not too great (as predicted by Hypothesis 5.3). As *Ideological Distance* increases, however, the gap between the hazard of a low vitality precedent being overruled and that of a high vitality precedent closes. For high values of *Ideological Distance*, the predicted hazard is larger for high vitality precedents. These predicted hazards again illustrate the argument we make. The most extreme form of negative interpretation, like

---

[7] The full or conditional coefficient for *Ideological Distance* is .0394 + (.0092 × *Precedent Vitality*). *Ideological Distance*, regardless of the size of *Precedent Vitality*, never has a statistically significant negative effect on the hazard of a precedent being overruled.

[8] All interval-level independent variables other than *Ideological Distance* and *Precedent Vitality* are either set one standard deviation above their mean if they are positively signed or one standard deviation below their mean if they are negatively signed. Dichotomous independent variables are set at the value which increases the probability of interpretation. The baseline hazard is set one standard deviation above its mean value. Therefore, these predicted hazards are for precedents that have an above-average risk of being overruled.

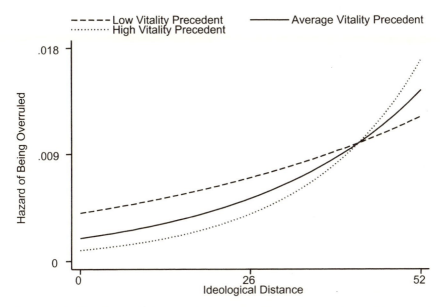

Figure 5.2. The effect of ideological distance and precedent vitality on the hazard of a precedent being overruled in a given year

Note: Ideological Distance is the absolute distance between the ideological position of the median member of the majority coalition in the precedent case and the median member of the Supreme Court in the given year. All interval-level independent variables other than *Ideological Distance* and *Precedent Vitality* are set one standard deviation above their mean if they are positively signed or one standard deviation below their mean if they are negatively signed. Dichotomous independent variables are set at the value that increases the probability of interpretation. The baseline hazard is set one standard deviation above its mean value. In short, these predicted hazards are for precedents that have an above-average risk of being overruled.

negative interpretation in general, is a function of policy preferences, precedent vitality, and the interaction between these two considerations.

The precedents discussed at the beginning of the chapter, *Aguilar* and *Spinelli*, can be mapped onto these predicted hazard curves. *Aguilar*, early in its existence, was ideologically quite close to the Court and of average vitality.[9] Thus, the hazard of this precedent being overruled was very low, somewhere on the leftmost part of the curve depicted with a solid line. Shortly after *Spinelli* was decided (1969), the Court shifted in a more conservative direction in the area of criminal procedure. With this

[9] For the first five years of *Aguilar*'s existence, the average ideological distance between the precedent and the median member of the Court was 3.1.

shift, the ideological distance between these two relatively liberal precedents and the Court increased. By 1983, the year these precedents were
overruled, the gap between the legal policy set by *Aguilar* and *Spinelli*
and the preferences of the Court was considerable, placing them approximately at the point at which the three predicted hazard curves inter-
sect.[10] Both precedents had a somewhat below-average level of vitality
by this point, but, given the level of ideological distance (high but not ex-
tremely high), this had little effect on their hazard of being overruled. If
they had not been overruled in 1983 and the distance between the precedents and the Court had continued to increase, then the hazard of them
being overruled would have also increased, although not at the same rate
as for a high vitality precedent.

The predicted hazards in figure 5.2 are most consistent with the first
theoretical scenario presented in chapter 2's figure 2.2. As seen in figure
5.2, the Court is more likely to overrule ideologically distant precedents
that are highly vital.[11] These results are basically consistent with those
for negative interpretation presented in chapter 4 and seem to suggest that
when the Court overrules precedent the effect of vitality may be somewhat more a function of the justices' desire to make the existing body of
precedent more compatible with their policy preferences than concerns
regarding the need to maximize the legitimacy of new policy choices. If
the justices were more concerned with maximizing legitimacy, then we
would expect to find that a precedent with a high level of vitality would
always be less likely to be overruled, regardless of whether the Court dis-
likes the precedent.

There may not appear to be a particularly substantial difference across
the three predicted hazard curves in figure 5.2, and all of the hazard rates
are quite small in size. We should point out, however, that small variations in the hazard rate can lead to significant changes in the predicted
duration of a precedent's survival. To illustrate this point, we graph the
predicted survival functions for four different scenarios (see figure 5.3).
A survival function is defined as the probability of surviving beyond time
t. In our context, the survival function is the probability of the precedent
not having been overruled by year *y*.

Each of the four scenarios in figure 5.3 corresponds with a point on
one of the predicted hazard functions in figure 5.2.[12] For example, the
survival function depicted as a solid line in figure 5.3 is derived from the
hazard associated with a high vitality precedent that is fully compatible

[10] *Ideological Distance* equaled 40.6 and 41.2 for *Aguilar* and *Spinelli*, respectively.

[11] The effect of *Precedent Vitality*, is not, however, statistically distinguishable from zero
for this range of the data.

[12] In this figure, however, the baseline hazard is not held constant at one value. It is al-
lowed to vary based on the value of *y* (i.e, the age of the precedent).

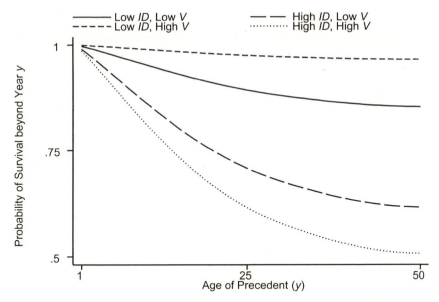

Figure 5.3. Predicted survival functions for the overruling of precedent

Note: V represents the vitality of the precedent and *ID* represents the ide-ological distance between the Court and the precedent. All interval-level inde-pendent variables other than *Ideological Distance* and *Precedent Vitality* are set one standard deviation above their mean if they are positively signed or one standard deviation below their mean if they are negatively signed. Dichotomous independent variables are set at the value that increases the probability of inter-pretation. The baseline hazard rate varies as a function of y, according to the recovered estimate of this rate.

with the Court in year y (i.e., *Ideological Distance* equals zero). In other words, this curve represents the probability of survival for a precedent whose hazard rate consists of the first point of the "high vitality" curve in figure 5.2. This is the lowest predicted hazard in figure 5.2, and, nec-essarily, this hazard corresponds with the survival curve with the shal-lowest downward slope. The difference between this survival function and the one represented by the medium-length dashed line is that the lat-ter is for a low vitality precedent. The two predicted survival functions for precedents for which *Ideological Distance* is high also then vary based on whether vitality is high (two standard deviations above the mean) or low (two standard deviations below the mean). The grimmest survival curve is that for high-vitality precedents that are ideologically distant from the Court. For these precedents, the probability of surviving longer than 50 years without being overruled is just over 50%.

The four survival functions in figure 5.3 illustrate the point that fairly small variations in the hazard of a precedent being overruled can lead to substantial differences in the probability of a precedent surviving over time without being overruled. The reader should not, however, make the mistake of inferring from these survival curves that *Ideological Distance* has a greater effect on precedent survival than *Precedent Vitality* because in this figure the former variable varies from its minimum to maximum value while the latter does not.

The Control Variables

Turning now to the results for the control variables included in the Cox model, it is apparent that the coefficient estimates for most of these variables conform to expectations. Two of the control variables are included because past studies suggest that they affect the likelihood of a precedent being treated negatively. The negative and statistically significant coefficient for *Voting Margin in Precedent* indicates that the more justices in the majority for the precedent-setting case, the lower the hazard of the precedent being overruled in any given subsequent year of its existence. In other words, 9–0 decisions are less likely to be overruled than 5–4 decisions. This result comports with what the justices themselves have said about the overruling of precedent. Rehnquist, for instance, states in *Payne v. Tennessee* (1991) that the Court is more likely to overrule a precedent decided by "the narrowest of margins" (501 U.S. 808, 829). However, when comparing this result with those in chapter 4, it appears that the justices are simply more likely to interpret a precedent, either positively or negatively, when the precedent case's majority coalition was smaller.

The estimate for *Concurring Opinions in Precedent* is in the expected direction (positive), but we cannot reject the null hypothesis that this coefficient is actually zero. Thus, there is not much support here for the contention that special concurring opinions weaken the precedent and make it more vulnerable to being overruled by a subsequent Court.

The rest of the control variables are included in the model because they are indicators of precedent salience or relevance and thus should predict the likelihood of a precedent being interpreted in any manner, including being overruled. The results of the Cox model reveal that the total number of previous interpretations of the precedent, the breadth of the precedent, and the amount of amicus participation in the precedent case increase the risk of a precedent being overruled in a given year. The extent to which the legal issue dealt with in the precedent is on the Court's agenda in a given year also has a positive effect on the hazard of the precedent being overruled in that year.

As demonstrated by the positive and significant estimate for *Constitu-*

tional Precedent, constitutional precedents are more likely to be overruled than precedents involving statutory interpretation. In both scholarly writings and Court opinions (see Ginsberg 1990, 144–45; *Payne v. Tennessee* 1991, 828; Rehnquist 1986, 350; Scalia 1994, 38), justices essentially make the claim that they are freer to overrule a constitutional precedent because, absent a new constitutional amendment, only the Court can correct problematic constitutional precedents. As Justice Powell notes, the same is not true for statutory decisions: "stare decisis should operate with special vigor in statutory cases because Congress has the power to pass new legislation correcting any statutory decision by the Court that Congress deems erroneous" (1990, 287). In a sense, our results here support the existence of this norm and suggest that the justices are, in fact, more prone to overrule a constitutional precedent than a statutory precedent. But, when considering the results of chapter 4, it appears that constitutional precedents are simply more likely to be interpreted, either positively or negatively. In other words, constitutional precedents may be more likely to be overruled than statutory precedents, but they are also more likely to be followed.

CONCLUSION

The overruling of precedent is the most severe and dramatic form of legal interpretation. The results of our analysis of the overruling of precedent, however, indicate that it is driven by the same set of factors that influence the likelihood of the Supreme Court interpreting a precedent in a generally negative manner. Our empirical results, in fact, are again quite supportive of our hypotheses regarding the interactive effect of precedent vitality and the ideological distance between the precedent and the Court. As ideological distance increases, the hazard or likelihood of a precedent being overruled also increases. But this effect is conditioned by the extent to which the precedent is vital.

This chapter therefore offers further support for our argument that precedent provides the justices with opportunities and constraints. Existing precedent represents a powerful opportunity for the justices as they seek to shape law consistent with their policy preferences. Thus, ideological considerations play a key role in the justices' choice to overrule a case. In addition, the legal vitality of a precedent plays an important role here, with the justices paying special attention to how vital a precedent is as they decide whether to overrule it.

We believe it is important that the results we find when analyzing the overruling of precedent comport with both our theory and our results in chapter 4 regarding the negative interpretation of precedent. Not only does this lend further support to our theory, but it also can be interpreted as validating the results of the last chapter. In the last chapter, we utilized *Shepard's Citations* to determine whether a precedent had been treated negatively in a given year. Here, the dependent variable, the overruling of precedent, is coded according to the scheme designed by Brenner and Spaeth (1995). The similarity in results across the two different measurements of the dependent variable suggests that our theory has explanatory power and that model estimation results are not sensitive to different specifications of the dependent variable.

CHAPTER SIX

The Interpretation of Precedent
in Majority Opinions

IN THE PRIOR TWO CHAPTERS, we sought to explain the interpretation of Supreme Court precedent over time. Once the Court sets a precedent, when and how will the Court interpret the precedent in subsequent years? Consistent with our theoretical model, the data analyses in chapters 4 and 5 show that the way in which the Court interprets a precedent over time depends on the relationship between the legal vitality of the precedent and the ideological distance between the Court and the precedent.

In this chapter, we ask a somewhat different question. When deciding a particular case (what we term a treatment case), how does the Court choose to interpret existing precedents? Instead of looking at how the Court treats precedents over time, we here examine why, in a given case, the Court interprets precedents either positively or negatively. We thus shift the unit of analysis from the precedent (used in chapters 4 and 5) to the treatment case.

For example, in *United States v. Felix* (1992) the Court faced the issue of the Double Jeopardy Clause's application to successive prosecutions involving the same underlying criminal conduct. Felix was convicted first in Missouri and then in Oklahoma for conduct related to manufacturing illegal drugs. In both trials the prosecution used much of Felix's same underlying conduct to prove their allegations. The Court of Appeals for the Tenth Circuit reversed Felix's conviction on various counts from the Oklahoma indictment as violating the Constitution's Double Jeopardy Clause. This decision was based on Brennan's opinion for the Court in *Grady v. Corbin* (1990), which held that the Double Jeopardy Clause bars subsequent prosecution where the government must prove conduct for which the defendant has already been convicted. For purposes of the Eighth Amendment, the Court defined the concept of "same offense" as "same conduct" in order to provide greater protection to defendants subject to successive prosecutions (McCune 1995).

In *Felix*, the Supreme Court reversed the lower court's decision and in the process interpreted two of its prior cases. First, the Court negatively treated *Grady* and rejected the lower court's reading of it. According to the Court (503 U.S. 378, 388): "Taken out of context, and read literally, this language [in *Grady*] supports the defense of double jeopardy. But we decline to read the language so expansively, because of the context in which *Grady* arose and because of difficulties which have already arisen in its interpretation." The Court created an exception to *Grady's* same conduct test to allow prosecution for a substantive crime and prosecution for criminal conspiracy charges under the same underlying conduct. It justified this narrowing of *Grady's* reach with cases decided prior to it. In particular, the Court relied upon and positively interpreted *United States v. Bauer* (1947), where the Court had ruled that criminal conduct and conspiracy to commit the same criminal conduct are separate and distinct offenses. Why did the Court in the *Felix* case (the treatment case in this context) opt to interpret the *Grady* precedent negatively and *Bauer* positively? This is a case-specific version of the general question we hope to answer.

This chapter will allow us to cross-validate the empirical results presented in chapters 4 and 5. Those data analyses confirm our theoretical predictions for the Court's treatment of precedent over time. If we can corroborate those results with evidence derived from a different research design, one in which the unit of analysis is the treatment case, then we have even greater support for the explanatory capability of our theoretical model. Indeed, one way that scientific evidence accumulates for a given theoretical point of view is when multiple studies employ different research designs and come to similar conclusions.

Hypotheses

We lay out our theoretical argument in detail in chapter 2; here we apply the propositions developed there to the Court's decision to interpret precedent in a particular case. Our model posits that the justices interpret precedent based on the desire to influence the extant body of Court precedent and to legitimize new policy outcomes. Both of these motivations relate to the justices' overarching interest in setting legal policy that will cause distributional effects they prefer. Based on these incentives and the resulting propositions in chapter 2, we have six specific predictions regarding the interpretation of precedent in a treatment case:

> *Hypothesis 6.1:* The greater the ideological distance between a precedent and the justices deciding a treatment case, the smaller the probability that the Court will positively interpret the precedent in the treatment case (see Proposition 2.1).

> *Hypothesis 6.2:* The more vital a precedent is when a treatment case is decided, the smaller the negative effect of ideologi-

cal distance on the probability of the precedent being positively treated in the treatment case (see Proposition 2.2).

Hypothesis 6.3: *The vitality of the precedent when a treatment case is decided will exert a positive effect on the probability of the precedent being interpreted positively in the treatment case, if the precedent is ideologically distant from the Court (see Proposition 2.3).*

Hypothesis 6.4: *The greater the ideological distance between a precedent and the justices deciding a treatment case, the greater the probability that the Court will negatively interpret the precedent in the treatment case (see Proposition 2.4).*

Hypothesis 6.5: *The more vital a precedent is when a treatment case is decided, the larger the positive effect of ideological distance on the probability of the precedent being negatively interpreted in the treatment case (see Proposition 2.5).*

Hypothesis 6.6: *The vitality of a precedent when a treatment case is decided will exert a negative effect on the probability of the precedent being interpreted negatively in the treatment case, if the precedent is ideologically close to the Court (see Proposition 2.6).*

DATA AND METHODS

To examine how the Court interprets existing precedent in particular treatment cases, we begin by defining our sample of treatment cases. We selected for study all orally argued opinions (full opinion, judgment of the Court, and *per curiam*) decided in the 1991, 1995, and 1999 terms of the Court (256 cases). These are the treatment cases in our analysis, meaning they are the cases in which the Court can interpret precedent.

We then identify existing precedents available to be interpreted in each of these treatment cases. There are a number of ways one could identify existing precedent for a case. One could, for example, define the set of precedents for a treatment case as the precedents cited in the litigant or amici briefs (see Spriggs and Hansford 2002). While it is not unreasonable to assume that interested actors would cite relevant cases in their briefs, it turns out that such a research design misses approximately 10% of all cases actually interpreted by the Court. Thus, this approach is underinclusive. One could alternatively define the set of precedents as prior cases falling within the same issue area as the treatment case, such as First Amendment cases (see McGuire and Mackuen 2001). This research design will also miss precedents that the Court interprets, since the Court can and does interpret precedents from one issue area when deciding cases in another. In fact, of the precedents treated by the Court in the data used in this chapter, 27.1% of them were in issue areas different from those at stake in the treatment cases that interpreted them.[1]

To avoid excluding precedents actually interpreted by the Court, or at risk of being interpreted, we define the set of precedents available to be interpreted by a treatment case as all orally argued Supreme Court cases decided beginning with the 1946 term and ending on the same day the treatment case is decided.[2] The unit of analysis is thus the treatment case–precedent dyad, meaning that there is an observation for each precedent for each treatment case.

We do not include precedents decided before the 1946 term because we do not have data on their interpretation at the Court over time. It is important for us to point out that this exclusion does not result in selection bias, but it does mean that we can only generalize to precedents decided beginning in the 1946 term.

As an example, consider *Neal v. United States*, which the Court decided on January 22, 1996. The set of precedents for this treatment case includes all precedents decided from the start of the 1946 term up to and including January 22, 1996. There are 5,979 precedents in our data that were decided prior to this case; our task is to explain which ones the Court interprets in a positive or negative fashion. For *Neal*, there is an observation in our data for each of these 5,979 precedents. This research design results in a total of 1,521,288 observations for our 256 treatment cases.[3]

---

[1] We use Spaeth's 12 broad issue areas to make this determination, and consider a treatment case and a precedent to be in the same broad issue area if they have any one issue area in common.

[2] As in our other analyses in this book, we examine all orally argued full opinion, *per curiam*, and judgments of the Court.

[3] This design results in a large number of observations, and as such the confidence intervals for our point estimates will be precise. While such a large dataset raises the likelihood of our finding a statistically significant effect if one actually exists, it *does not* raise the likelihood of a Type I error (i.e., finding an effect when one does not exist). One must always be concerned with the magnitude of an effect and not just whether it is statistically significant. In a large dataset, when one is better able to detect statistically significant, but perhaps substantively small, effects, this concern is even more pronounced. We will therefore provide specific estimates and graphical illustrations for the effect sizes demonstrated by our empirical models.

To measure our dependent variable, we once again turn to *Shepard's Citations* and employ the coding rules specified in chapter 3. We designate situations in which the treatment case "Followed" a precedent as positive interpretation of that precedent. We consider any precedent that was "Distinguished," "Criticized," "Limited," "Questioned," or "Overruled" as being negatively interpreted by the treatment case. The dependent variable for the positive interpretation model equals one if the Court in the treatment case positively interpreted the precedent, and zero otherwise. Likewise, the dependent variable for the negative interpretation model equals one if the Court negatively interpreted the precedent in the treatment case. We estimate our models as logit models, and since the same precedents appear multiple times across the treatment cases, we use robust standard errors that allow for the residuals associated with a precedent to be correlated.[4]

Obviously, our data include situations in which a given precedent may not be at all relevant for the given treatment case. To ensure that all precedents that could be interpreted by the Court are included in our data, however, we chose to err on the side of being overinclusive. To account for this issue, our statistical models incorporate a series of control variables that capture the relevance of a precedent for a treatment case.

Independent Variables

We construct the three independent variables of theoretical significance in a manner similar to the measures in chapters 4 and 5. We measure *Ideological Distance* as the absolute difference between the issue-specific ideology of the median of the majority voting coalition for the precedent and the issue-specific ideology of the median member of the majority voting coalition in the treatment case.[5] *Precedent Vitality* is the difference between the prior number of positive and negative interpretations of the precedent by the Supreme Court in years prior to the one in which the treatment case was decided. Our theoretical predictions also require us to include the interaction term based on these two variables, *Ideological*

---

[4] These dependent variables are highly skewed, and King and Zeng (2001) suggest accounting for this feature of dichotomous data with a rare events logit model. With our data, however, the rare events logit model produces results that are essentially the same as those obtained from a traditional logit model. We therefore present the traditional logit model results.

[5] In these data, *Ideological Distance* has a larger range (0 to 74.4) than in the previous chapters. Here, a treatment case's majority coalition median is compared with a precedent case's majority coalition median. In previous chapters, the median justice on the Court for a given year is compared with a precedent case's majority coalition median.

Distance × *Precedent Vitality.* See chapter 4 for detailed descriptions of the measurement of these variables.

In addition to these variables, we include three types of controls. First, we incorporate the precedent-specific control variables utilized in chapters 4 and 5: *Concurring Opinions in Precedent, Voting Margin in Precedent, Total Prior Interpretations, Overruled Precedent, Breadth of Precedent, Constitutional Precedent, Amici Filings in Precedent, Media Coverage of Precedent, Per Curiam Precedent, Age of Precedent*, and *Age of Precedent Squared.*[6] Descriptions of the measurement of each of these variables are located in chapter 4.

Second, our data include precedents that may be more or less legally relevant for a treatment case, and we control for this feature of the data with five variables that capture this type of relevance. The first variable, *Number of Citing Briefs*, is measured as the number of litigant and amici briefs filed in the treatment case that cite the precedent. The larger the number of briefs that cite the precedent, the more likely it is relevant for the treatment case. We gathered these data from the "Table of Authorities" section of all briefs on the merits filed in the treatment cases.

The next four variables for legal relevance measure similarities between a precedent and the treatment case. *Same Broad Issue* is coded as one if the precedent and treatment case share the same broad legal issue area (e.g., First Amendment, Economic Activity). *Same Narrow Issue* equals one if the precedent and the treatment case share the same narrow issue area.[7] The next indicator, *Same Authority*, equals one if the precedent and treatment case are decided under the same authority (e.g., constitutional interpretation, statutory interpretation), as coded by Spaeth (1995, 2001). The final measure of relevance, *Same Legal Provision*, equals one if a precedent and a treatment case deal with the same specific legal provision (i.e., the constitutional provision, statute, court rule, or treaty at issue), as coded by Spaeth (1995, 2001).

Third, we control for the possibility of treatment case–based effects

---

[6] In chapters 4 and 5 we used a variable, *Court Agenda*, to control for whether the issue area of a precedent was still active on the Court's agenda. There is no need to include that variable in these models because we have more specific relevance measures that specifically tap the relationship between each precedent and each treatment case.

[7] Spaeth (1995, 2001) identifies 12 broad issue areas: Criminal Procedure, First Amendment, Civil Rights, Due Process, Privacy, Attorneys, Unions, Economic Activity, Judicial Power, Federalism, Interstate Relations, and Federal Taxation. In addition, Spaeth identifies approximately 260 narrow issue areas representing the context in which the broad legal issue in the case appears. For example, within First Amendment cases, Spaeth identifies a variety of specific issues, including free exercise of religion, establishment of religion, government aid to religious schools, etc. Spaeth's coding scheme allows a case to fall in multiple broad and narrow issue areas, and we code a precedent and treatment case as sharing the same broad or narrow issue area if they have any one area in common.

due to the salience or breadth of a treatment case. Treatment cases that are more salient or have greater breadth may be more likely to interpret a larger number of precedents. We use *Amici Filings in Treatment Case* to account for the salience of a treatment case, and we gather these data from Gibson (1997). Unlike in chapters 4 and 5, we do not include a variable for media coverage of a treatment case. It is an ex post variable in that it measures media coverage that takes place after a case has been decided.[8] We include two variables for the breadth of a treatment case. First, we use a variable analogous to the one that accounts for the breadth of a precedent, *Breadth of Treatment Case*. Second, we control for breadth using the total number of Supreme Court precedents cited in the litigant and amici briefs (*Number of Precedents Cited in Briefs*).

RESULTS

In these treatment cases, the Supreme Court interpreted 247 precedents positively and 211 precedents negatively. The average treatment case interpreted 1.7 precedents either positively or negatively, and this number varies from a low of 0 to a high of 21. These data serve to reinforce the message from the longitudinal data presented in chapter 3—the Court's interpretation of prior cases is not an overly frequent event.[9] Nonetheless, we continue to argue (and empirically demonstrate in chapter 7) that when the Court does interpret precedent it is a meaningful event. The results of the models explaining the interpretation of precedent in a given case are provided in table 6.1.

The Results of the Positive Interpretation Model

Of the three predictions for positive interpretation, the data provide partial support for two of them. Our first expectation (Hypothesis 6.1) was that the probability of positive interpretation would decline as the justices deciding a treatment case became more ideologically opposed to a precedent. The negative and significant coefficient for *Ideological Distance* offers support for this idea.[10] For instance, in the case example

---

[8] It is possible that the way in which the Court interprets precedent will influence media coverage, rather than vice versa.

[9] Prior research indicates that the Court cites approximately 12 to 15 precedents in each opinion (Johnson 1985; Landes and Posner 1976), but it only substantively interprets about 20% of those citations. Thus, like prior studies, our data show that the Court legally interprets relatively few precedents in an opinion.

[10] The conditional effect of *Ideological Distance* is negative for all values of *Precedent Vitality* and is statistically significant for values of *Precedent Vitality* greater than or equal to zero and less than or equal to one (73.5% of the data).

TABLE 6.1
Logit Models of the Supreme Court's Interpretation of Precedent in a Given Case

Independent Variable	Positive Interpretation Coefficient (Robust S.E.)	Negative Interpretation Coefficient (Robust S.E.)
Ideological Distance (*ID*)	−.0148 (.0073)*	.0156 (.0071)*
Precedent Vitality (*V*)	.1223 (.0672)	−.1466 (.0783)*
Ideological Distance × Vitality (*ID* × *V*)	−.0008 (.0032)	.0091 (.0025)*
Control Variables:		
Concurring Opinions in Precedent	−.0384 (.1195)	.0678 (.1338)
Voting Margin in Precedent	−.0694 (.0285)	−.0320 (.0275)
Total Prior Interpretations	.1250 (.0153)*	.1088 (.0222)*
Breadth of Precedent	−.1206 (.1748)	.1891 (.1434)
Amici Filings in Precedent	.0363 (.0778)	−.1325 (.1023)
Media Coverage of Precedent	.2380 (.2016)	−.0883 (.2489)
Per Curiam Precedent	−2.171 (.8045)*	−.7517 (.5526)
Constitutional Precedent	−.1794 (.1796)	−.0491 (.1841)
Overruled Precedent	.5766 (.5419)	.6901 (.4537)
Age of Precedent	−.0715 (.0199)^	−.0399 (.0234)^
Age of Precedent Squared	.0004 (.0004)	−.0002 (.0005)
Number of Citing Briefs	.3050 (.0351)*	.2950 (.0336)*
Same Broad Issue	1.241 (.2109)*	1.481 (.2005)*
Same Narrow Issue	1.678 (.2727)*	1.328 (.2776)*
Same Legal Provision	1.960 (.2988)*	1.587 (.2794)*
Same Authority	.1308 (.1833)	.4923 (.1764)*
Amici Filings in Treatment Case	−.1381 (.1087)	−.3031 (.1361)
Breadth of Treatment Case	.8053 (.1805)*	.5101 (.2077)*
Number of Precedents Cited in Briefs	.0004 (.0010)	.0015 (.0011)
Constant	−8.647 (.3076)^	−9.706 (.3203)^
Number of Observations	1,521,288	1,521,288
Log Likelihood	−1541	−1532
Wald Test (Chi-square, 22 d.o.f.)	2116*	1703*

* $p \le .05$ (one-tailed test, for directional hypotheses), ^ $p \le .05$ (two-tailed test, for non-directional controls and constants).

with which we opened this chapter we see the majority coalition in *United States v. Felix* (1992) positively interprets *United States v. Bauer* (1947), a case that it preferred on ideological grounds.[11]

However, the data do not provide confirmation for Hypothesis 6.2, which predicts that the influence of the ideological distance between the justices and a precedent would be conditional on the vitality of the precedent. The coefficient for the interaction between *Ideological Distance* and *Precedent Vitality* is not in the predicted direction. This is the only analysis in this book for which our expectations regarding this particular relationship does not hold.

Figure 6.1 illustrates the effect of *Ideological Distance*.[12] The curves represent the predicted probabilities of positive interpretation for three types of precedent: a precedent with below-average vitality (two standard deviations below the mean), a precedent with average vitality, and a precedent with above-average vitality (two standard deviations above the mean). As expected, the slopes for all three curves are negative, indicating the Court's decreasing propensity to positively interpret precedents with which they disagree on policy grounds. But, contrary to Hypothesis 6.2, we do not see the curves begin to flatten out for precedents that are more vital. In other words, in this one instance we do not see the vitality of a precedent acting to attenuate the negative effect of ideological distance on the likelihood of the Court positively interpreting a precedent.

Our model's third prediction is that *Precedent Vitality* will have a positive effect on the probability of the Court interpreting a precedent positively, if the Court is ideologically opposed to the precedent. The data provide some support for this idea, as the conditional effect of *Precedent Vitality* is positive not only for high values of *Ideological Distance*, but for the entire range of the variable. But the conditional effect is statistically significant for only part of the range of values of *Ideological Distance*. Specifically, it is not statistically significant for values of *Ideological Distance* greater than its 81st percentile (29.3). We can therefore only conclude that *Precedent Vitality* increases the likelihood

---

[11] The ideological location of the majority voting coalition in *Felix* was 28.4, and the ideological location of *Bauer* (based on its majority voting coalition) was 38.3, yielding an *Ideological Distance* score of 9.9 (.6 standard deviations below the mean value of *Ideological Distance*).

[12] Because the likelihood of a treatment case positively interpreting the average precedent is very small, when generating this figure we set all control variables at one standard deviation above their mean if they increase the chance of positive interpretation and one standard deviation below their mean if they decrease it (we set dichotomous variables at zero or one depending on the direction of their coefficient). *Number of Citing Briefs* is set at 5, which is more than one standard deviation above its mean value, but far below the maximum value (29).

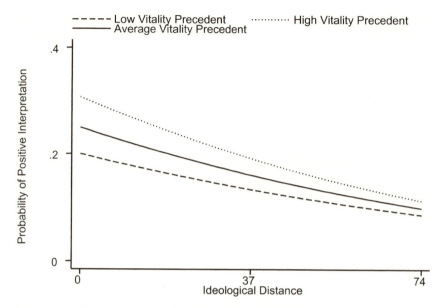

Figure 6.1. The influence of ideological distance and precedent vitality on the probability of a precedent being positively interpreted in a Supreme Court case

Note: Ideological Distance is the absolute distance between the ideological position of the median member of the majority coalition in the precedent case and the median member of the majority voting coalition in the treatment case. Control variables are set at one standard deviation above their mean if they increase the chance of positive interpretation and one standard deviation below their mean if they decrease it (with the exception of *Number of Citing Briefs*, which is set at 5). Dichotomous variables are set at zero or one depending on the direction of their coefficient. These probabilities thus correspond to a precedent with an above-average likelihood of being interpreted.

of a precedent being positively interpreted by the Court when a precedent is anywhere from moderately distant to very close to the Court, ideologically speaking.

Our theoretical model does not yield a prediction regarding the effect of *Precedent Vitality* when the Court is in agreement with a precedent (i.e., *Ideological Distance* is small), since the desire to legitimize new decisions (captured by b_4 in chapter 2) and the desire to affect the state of existing precedent ($-b_3$ in chapter 2) cut in opposite directions. The data here indicate that, for cases ideologically proximate to the justices deciding a treatment case, increases in *Precedent Vitality* raise the probability of positive interpretation. This particular result suggests that, when they interpret precedents positively, the legitimacy concern underlying the vitality of precedent is more important to the justices than the desire to shape existing precedent. This result is further evident in figure 6.1, where, for any given value of *Ideological Distance*, the Court is always more inclined to positively interpret precedents with greater vitality.

The Results of the Negative Interpretation Model

Our theory leads to three predictions regarding when a treatment case will negatively interpret a precedent, all of which find support in these data. As stated by Hypothesis 6.4, we expect the justices deciding a treatment case to be more likely to negatively interpret precedents that are ideologically distant from them. The positive and statistically significant coefficient for *Ideological Distance* provides initial evidence for this expectation. The data indicate that when *Precedent Vitality* equals zero, the justices in the majority in a treatment case are more likely to negatively interpret precedents with which they disagree on policy grounds. In *United States v. Felix* (1992), the case with which we opened this chapter, the majority coalition negatively interpreted *Grady v. Corbin* (1990), a precedent at odds with the preferences of the Rehnquist Court.[13] Indeed, the dissenting coalition in *Grady* became the majority coalition in *Felix* due in large part to the replacement of Justices Brennan and Marshall with, respectively, Justices Souter and Thomas.

Examination of the conditional effect of *Ideological Distance* [.0156 + (.0091 × *Precedent Vitality*)] reveals that the results mostly conform to our expectations. The conditional effect of *Ideological Distance* is, as expected, positive and statistically significant for values of *Precedent Vitality* greater than or equal to 0. But when *Precedent Vitality* is low (less than or equal to −2), the conditional effect of *Ideological Distance* becomes negative. This latter result is not consistent with Hypothesis 6.1. Nonetheless, the prediction that *Ideological Distance* increases the likelihood of the Court interpreting a precedent negatively is true for 78.7% of the data. We further claim, in Hypothesis 6.2, that the influence of *Ideological Distance* is enhanced for precedents that have a greater level of vitality. The positive and statistically significant coefficient for *Ideological Distance × Vitality* supports this argument. The more vital the precedent, the greater the effect of the justices' policy preferences on negative interpretation.

Our final hypothesis states that precedents that are more vital will be less likely to be negatively interpreted when they are ideologically close

---

[13] The majority coalition in *Felix* had an ideological location of 28.4 (quite conservative), while *Grady* had a score of 63.5 (quite liberal), making the value of *Ideological Distance* between the Court and this precedent 35.1 (1.4 standard deviations above the mean value of *Ideological Distance*).

to the justices deciding a treatment case. The coefficient for *Precedent Vitality* is negative and statistically significant and thus supports Hypothesis 6.6. By itself, it shows that when the justices deciding a treatment case are in complete agreement with a precedent (*Ideological Distance* = 0), the probability of negative interpretation decreases as *Precedent Vitality* increases.[14] This effect is produced by both the motivation to alter the current body of precedent and the need to legitimize new policy choices.

Our theoretical model does not predict the effect of the vitality of a precedent when the justices deciding a treatment case are in ideological opposition to the precedent. The data reveal that *Precedent Vitality* is positive and statistically significant for values of *Ideological Distance* above 25.8 (which is near the 75th percentile for this variable). When a precedent is disliked by the justices in the majority of a treatment case, the precedent is more likely to be negatively interpreted if the precedent is particularly vital. This result allows us to speak to the two somewhat competing aspects of legal vitality contained in our model. The data show that when deciding to negatively interpret a precedent, the justices are motivated more by the desire to place their spin on existing precedents than the desire to avoid actions that might reduce the legitimacy of new policy choices.

The most effective way to gauge the magnitude of these relationships is with a graphical representation. In figure 6.2, we plot the influence of *Ideological Distance* for three distinct values of *Precedent Vitality*.[15] This figure illustrates how the vitality of a precedent amplifies the positive effect of the ideological distance between a precedent and the justices in the majority in a treatment case. Ideologically distant precedents are more likely to be negatively interpreted if they have a high degree of vitality. Conversely, precedents that are perfectly aligned with the majority's preferences will be less likely to be treated negatively if they are vital. It is worth pointing out that we do not expect to see a downward sloping curve for the low vitality precedent. As vitality decreases, the positive effect of *Ideological Distance* should decrease, but not to the point that this effect becomes negative.

When comparing this figure to the hypothetical scenarios presented in chapter 2, it is clear that the empirical results regarding the decision to treat a precedent negatively most closely resemble the scenario (scenario 1) in which the motivation to influence the current body of precedent

---

[14] *Precedent Vitality* is negative and significant for values of *Ideological Distance* less than or equal to 3.0, which is at about the 10th percentile of *Ideological Distance*.

[15] These predicted probabilities are calculated in the same manner as they are for figure 6.1.

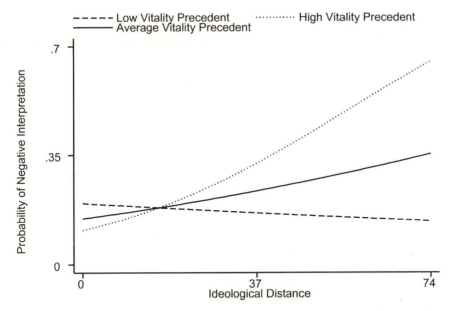

Figure 6.2. The influence of ideological distance and precedent vitality on the probability of a precedent being negatively interpreted in a Supreme Court case

Note: Ideological Distance is the absolute distance between the ideological position of the median member of the majority coalition in the precedent case and the median member of the majority voting coalition in the treatment case. Control variables are set at one standard deviation above their mean if they increase the chance of negative interpretation and one standard deviation below their mean if they decrease it (with the exception of *Number of Citing Briefs*, which is set at 5). Dichotomous variables are set at zero or one depending on the direction of their coefficient. These probabilities are thus associated with a precedent with an above-average likelihood of being interpreted.

outweighs concerns regarding the effect of negative interpretation on the Court's ability to legitimize new policy. This result is fairly consistent with what we find in chapters 4 and 5.

The Control Variables

Our empirical model includes three types of controls. The first set of variables accounts for characteristics of precedents that may affect how or whether a case will be interpreted positively or negatively. As a set, these variables do little to explain these dependent variables. While most of these variables are significant in chapters 4 and 5, only *Total Prior Interpretations* affects both the positive and negative interpretation of precedent in the analysis presented here. These results also suggest that per curiam precedents and older precedents are less likely to be positively interpreted in a given case.

The variables included to control for the relevance of a precedent for a treatment case appear to have much more explanatory power. Only one of these five variables across the two models (*Same Authority* in the Positive Interpretation model) fails to achieve statistical significance. In a given treatment case, the Court is more likely to interpret a precedent if the litigants and amici curiae reference the precedent in their briefs, the precedent dealt with the same issue at stake in the treatment case, and the treatment case involves the same legal provision as the precedent. Simply put, the Court is more likely to interpret legally relevant precedents when deciding a case, and this result, in a sense, indicates the importance of the norm of *stare decisis*. The Court has a strong tendency to deal with the precedents that are legally relevant, just as it tends to deal only with the legal issues that are presented by the litigants (see Epstein, Segal, and Johnson 1996).

The third set of variables controls for treatment case–specific effects. Our results here indicate that the broader the treatment case, the greater the probability of the Court interpreting any particular precedent. The other controls of this type are not statistically significant.

Comparing the Results

An obvious question to ask is how the results in this chapter compare to those from chapters 4 and 5. With the exception of the interaction term in the positive interpretation model, the results largely accord with those reported in prior chapters. Beginning with the negative interpretation model, we see that all three predictions receive empirical support across chapters 4, 5, and 6. One of the most effective ways to examine the comparability of the results is to compare figures 4.2 and 5.2 with figure 6.2. Most certainly, subtle differences exist. For example, *Precedent Vitality* is negative and statistically significant for a broader range of low values of *Ideological Distance* in chapters 4 and 5 than in chapter 6. Yet, what is most striking is that, despite the significant difference in the research designs between the prior two chapters and this one, the basic form of the relationship between negative treatment and our theoretical variables of interest, ideological distance, and precedent vitality, appears quite similar.

The degree of similarity is less pronounced for positive interpretation. While both analyses provide considerable support for our prediction regarding the effect of ideological distance, this chapter provides less support for our other two hypotheses. With regard to the vitality of precedent, the data analyses in chapters 4 and 5 provide clear support for our predictions. The results in this chapter, however, offer qualified support for Hypothesis 6.3. Specifically, the coefficient for *Precedent Vitality* is in the predicted direction for some, but not all, of the range of *Ideological Distance* for which we expect it to matter.

The most noticeable difference, of course, is that the data in this chapter do not confirm Hypothesis 6.2, while chapters 4 and 5 demonstrate considerable evidence for a conditional relationship between *Ideological Distance* and *Precedent Vitality*. This discrepancy is most evident in a comparison of figure 4.1 and figure 6.1. While the slope of the curves gets flatter as *Precedent Vitality* increases in figure 4.1—indicating that the influence of *Ideological Distance* is stronger for less vital precedents— we do not witness a corresponding effect in figure 6.1.

In addition, the results regarding the relative influence of the two components of the effect of precedent vitality are also reasonably similar across these chapters. With regard to positive interpretation, the data analysis in this chapter and chapter 4 indicates that legitimacy incentives may outweigh the desire to alter the current body of precedent. When considering the negative interpretation of precedent, the data here and in chapters 4 and 5 suggest that the latter motivation might dominate.

What do we infer from these results? Generally speaking, the evidence presented in this chapter further confirms our theoretical argument. Indeed, despite the significant difference in the two research designs, the results of the negative interpretation model are basically the same. The results for the positive interpretation model in this chapter are not as compelling as the data analysis in prior chapters. One reason for this disparity may be that the research design in this chapter is somewhat less powerful than the one we use in chapters 4 and 5. We say this for two reasons. First, this chapter's research design excludes precedents decided prior to 1946, and as a result misses interpretations in some of the treatment cases. Second, this research design requires one to define the set of precedents available to be interpreted in a treatment case. Doing so is no easy task. Our approach ensures that we do not exclude any treatments of the precedents in our analysis, but it inevitably leads to including precedents that are not relevant. We remain convinced that being overinclusive, as opposed to underinclusive, is the lesser evil, but this feature of the data may somewhat dampen the results.

CONCLUSION

The goal of this chapter was to explain how the Court interprets precedents positively or negatively in a given case. Our argument is that the

justices do so based on the interaction between their policy preferences
and the legal vitality of a precedent. As detailed in chapter 2, both of these
factors influence the interpretation of precedent because of the justices'
desire to set legal policy that will influence society in ways they prefer. As
the foregoing pages reveal, the data analysis in this chapter provides substantial support for our argument. This chapter therefore generally serves
to reinforce the results in chapters 4 and 5, though with certain caveats.

The data in this chapter further substantiate our central theoretical
claim that both the need to legitimize new policy choices and the desire
to affect existing legal policy motivate the justices' interpretation of precedent. There is an important interactive relationship between the justices' policy preferences and the legal vitality of a precedent. We see, first,
that the justices make these decisions based on their policy goals. For example, the justices are considerably more likely to negatively interpret a
precedent in a treatment case when that precedent is further from their
preferred policy. And this ideological motivation is further demonstrated
in the justices' enhanced propensity to negatively treat ideologically distant precedents that are more vital.

We also show that concerns over the need to legitimize current policy
choices influence legal development. This effect is most visible in the
model of positive interpretation, where the likelihood of the justices positively interpreting a precedent is always higher for more vital precedents. Based on our model, this pattern in the data can only be consistent with the justices taking into consideration legal vitality as a means
to promote a decision's legitimacy.

CHAPTER SEVEN

Lower Federal Court Responses to the Supreme Court's Interpretation of Precedent

AT THIS POINT, we have provided three distinct tests of our theoretical expectations regarding the interpretation of precedent at the U.S. Supreme Court. In this last empirical chapter, we examine the validity of a critical assumption underlying the hypotheses we have tested in the preceding chapters. Embedded in our theoretical model is an assumption that the behavior of a wide variety of decision makers can be influenced by the Court's decision to restrict or expand the meaning or applicability of a precedent. In other words, we have been working from the assumption that the Supreme Court's interpretation of its precedents is a meaningful activity in both a legal and political sense.

The Court's power to exert a wide-ranging influence over outcomes rests on its ability to affect the choices that both public officials and private citizens make. A body of previous research provides considerable evidence that Court precedents can have such effects. Studies indicate, for example, that the Court's opinions influence the behavior of private parties (e.g., Bond and Johnson 1982; Cooter, Marks, and Mnookin 1982; Dometrius and Sigelman 1988; Priest and Klein 1976) and the policy choices of federal bureaucratic agencies (e.g., Spriggs 1996, 1997; Wood and Anderson 1993), the U.S. Congress (Martin 2001), and state legislatures (e.g., Glick 1994).[1]

Lower court judges comprise one notable subset of decision makers that, at least in theory, should almost always be affected by the Supreme Court's treatment of precedent. The scholarly literature generally suggests that lower courts are responsive to the Supreme Court. Research shows that lower federal courts tend to follow the Court's legal rulings (e.g., Benesh 2002; Benesh and Reddick 2002; Johnson 1979, 1987; Klein 2002; Songer 1988; Songer and Haire 1992; Songer and Sheehan 1990; Wahlbeck 1998) and mirror the Court's decision trends (Songer

---

[1] Supreme Court decisions can also affect public opinion (Hoekstra 2003; Johnson and Martin 1998) and the national agenda (Flemming, Bohte, and Wood 1997). However, Court decisions may not always lead to wide-ranging consequences (see Rosenberg 1991).

1987; Songer, Segal, and Cameron 1994).[2] For example, Wahlbeck (1998) shows that after the Supreme Court ruled that the federal common law of public nuisance was preempted by congressional legislation, lower courts stopped expanding that doctrine. Benesh and Reddick (2002) demonstrate that lower courts generally stop relying on a precedent if the Supreme Court has overruled the precedent. None of this research, however, examines whether other types of interpretation of precedent influence how lower courts use precedent.

We wish to extend these analyses and assess our assumption that the Supreme Court's interpretation of its precedents matters by investigating whether lower federal courts respond to how the Court has interpreted a precedent. The results of this analysis should be relevant for the literature on the development of the law at the Court as well as the study of lower court compliance with Supreme Court precedent. While the above-discussed research finds that lower courts tend to comply with the Supreme Court, much of it is based on analyses of specific areas of the law (e.g., Songer and Haire 1992; Wahlbeck 1998), a small number of cases (e.g., Johnson 1987), or particularly salient precedents (e.g., Benesh and Reddick 2002; Songer and Sheehan 1990). With our analysis, we intend to show more generally that lower courts respond to the Court's changing interpretations of its precedents.

This chapter proceeds as follows. We begin with a brief discussion of why lower courts might respond to the Supreme Court's interpretations of its precedents. In order to test whether lower court usage of Court precedent changes as a function of subsequent Court interpretations, we then empirically estimate a trio of event count models. The chapter concludes with a discussion of the implications of our analysis.

LOWER COURT RESPONSIVENESS

The prior chapters in this book theoretically and empirically demonstrate that the vitality of a Supreme Court precedent affects how the Supreme Court interprets it. We define precedent vitality as the legal authority or weight of a case, as determined by the Supreme Court's prior interpretation of it. The meaning of a precedent is thus not fixed but can change over time as the Court interprets it in subsequent cases. If, for example, the Court treats a case positively, by following it and declaring that it is good law, then the authority of the case is enhanced. If the

[2] Other studies also examine patterns of precedent usage across courts that reside at the same level in the judicial hierarchy. For example, Caldeira (1985, 1988) investigates how one state supreme court uses the precedent set by another state supreme court.

Court negatively treats a case by limiting it to its facts or indicating that it does not apply to a new factual scenario, then the reach of a case may be diminished.

Theoretically, lower courts have the same legitimacy incentives as the Supreme Court to respond to the vitality of a Supreme Court precedent. Lower courts need to promote the legitimacy of their decisions in order to ensure that their policies are efficacious. The importance of legitimacy for American courts derives both from the social expectation that they justify their decisions based on legally relevant criteria (see Friedman et al. 1981; Johnson 1987; Maltz 1988) and from their lack of implementation powers (see Epstein and Knight 1998). Judges therefore often justify their decisions based on precedent as a way to connect new policies with past rules of law (Phelps and Gates 1996; Knight and Epstein 1996). By doing so, judges can foster the legitimacy of their opinions and thus enhance their prospects for influencing distributional outcomes.

As made clear in chapter 2, however, not all precedents enjoy the same level of legal vitality (Aldisert 1990; Johnson 1987; Peczenik 1997; Ulmer 1959). The U.S. Supreme Court can affect the legal authority of a precedent by interpreting it in subsequent cases. Positive interpretation enhances the legal vitality of a case, while negative interpretation can decrease its legal weight (Landes and Posner 1976; Stern 1989; Wald 1995). Importantly, precedents that possess greater legal weight are better suited for justifying decisions than cases with less vitality. As a result, we expect lower court judges to be responsive to the vitality of a precedent.

Lower courts also have a second type of incentive to respond to changes in the vitality of a Court precedent. As recognized by many scholars, lower court judges may seek, at least in part, to avoid being reversed on appeal (e.g., Baum 1997; Songer, Segal, and Cameron 1994; cf. Klein and Hume 2003). Since the U.S. Supreme Court can reverse lower court decisions, lower courts may be particularly sensitive to changes in the vitality of a Supreme Court precedent. The Court's negative treatment of a precedent should signal the lower courts that the Court is not enamored with the precedent and thus may not expect lower courts to apply the precedent in a broad or extensive manner. Likewise, positive treatment of a precedent by the Court signals that lower courts need to consider adhering to this precedent when deciding relevant cases.

Thus, it is theoretically reasonable to expect lower courts to be responsive to the Supreme Court's interpretation of a precedent. Both the need to maintain legitimacy and the desire to avoid being reversed by the Court will lead lower court usage of precedent to be influenced by the vitality of the precedent. More specifically, we test the following three hypotheses regarding lower court usage of Supreme Court precedent:

Hypothesis 7.1: *The more vital a Supreme Court precedent (i.e., the more often the Court has treated it positively than negatively), the more often lower courts will cite the precedent.*

Hypothesis 7.2: *The frequency with which lower courts treat a Court precedent positively (i.e., follow the precedent) will increase as the vitality of the precedent increases.*

Hypothesis 7.3: *The more vital a Supreme Court precedent, the less frequently lower courts will treat the precedent in a negative fashion (e.g., distinguish or limit the precedent).*

DATA AND METHODS

To test the effect of the vitality of Supreme Court precedent on lower court usage of it, we examine lower federal court usage of 200 U.S. Supreme Court precedents randomly selected from the 6,363 U.S. Supreme Court precedents we analyze in earlier chapters. We gather the data for our dependent variables from *Shepard's Citations*. Specifically, we identify all the instances, from the year a precedent was decided through 2001, in which a federal district or appeals court cited the precedent, treated the precedent positively, or treated the precedent negatively.[3] We code any precedent that *Shepard's* labels as "Cited by," "Explained," or "Harmonized" as a citation to the precedent.[4] Following *Shepard's*, we consider any lower court decision that "Followed" one of these precedent as treating the precedent positively. We code any situation in which the lower courts "Distinguished," "Criticized," "Limited," or "Questioned" one of these precedents as negative treatment.[5]

---

[3] We do not include citations and treatments in decisions handed down by specialized federal courts, such as the Court of Appeals for the Federal Circuit.

[4] "Explained" and "Harmonized" represent "neutral" forms of legal interpretation (i.e., they are neither positive nor negative treatment) and we thus include them with citations. Explained indicates that "the citing opinion clarifies, interprets, construes or otherwise annotates the decision in the cited case" (Shepard's 1993, 16), and Harmonized means "that the cases differ in some way; however, the court has found a way to reconcile and bring into harmony the apparent inconsistency" (Shepard's 1993, 18). If we exclude neutral treatments from the citation count, *Precedent Vitality* remains positive and statistically significant.

[5] See chapter 3 for further discussion of the mechanics and reliability of *Shepard's Citations*. *Shepard's* does not allow the category of Overruled to be used for lower court treatments of higher courts because lower courts do not have the authority to overrule the precedents of a higher court (Shepard's 1993, 20–21). If a citing court is without authority to overrule, then *Shepard's* uses the Questioned code for such behavior.

We then aggregate all lower federal court treatments of a precedent by year, yielding a dataset in which the unit of analysis is the precedent-year. That is, for each of the 200 Supreme Court precedents in our sample there is an observation for the year the precedent was established and every subsequent year through 2001 (for a total of 5,949 observations). For a precedent set in 1980, for example, there are 22 observations in the data. For each of these observations, the number of lower federal court citations, positive treatments of the precedent, and negative treatments of the precedent are recorded. All three dependent variables vary across precedents and across time.

To test our hypotheses regarding the effect of precedent vitality on lower federal court usage of precedent, we estimate three negative binomial regression models, which are a type of event count model. We choose to use this particular type of event count model because it allows for overdispersed data (i.e., the variance exceeds the mean), whereas the Poisson regression model assumes that the data are equidispersed (i.e., the conditional mean and variance are equal) (see Cameron and Trivedi 1998; Long 1997).

In the first model, the dependent variable is the number of lower federal court cases citing the precedent in a given year. The dependent variable in the second model is the number of lower court decisions that positively treat the precedent in a given year, while in the third model it is the number of negative treatments in each year.

Independent Variables

The vitality of a Supreme Court precedent constitutes the independent variable of primary interest. To measure precedent vitality, we use *Shepard's Citations* to count the number of times the Supreme Court's majority opinions interpreted a precedent in a positive or negative manner up to the year prior to the one under consideration.[6] We then take the difference between the number of prior positive and negative interpretations. Positive scores indicate that the Court has interpreted the precedent positively more often than negatively in previous years, while negative scores indicate the opposite. This is the same measure of *Precedent Vitality* that we have used in the previous chapters.

We expect *Precedent Vitality* to have a positive coefficient in the citation and positive treatment models. Supreme Court precedents with a higher level of vitality should be cited and followed more often than precedents with a lower level of vitality. In the negative treatment model, we expect *Precedent Vitality* to have a negative coefficient, as lower federal

---

[6] We exclude from this count any memorandum opinion that interpreted a precedent.

courts should be less likely to treat a Court precedent negatively if it has a higher level of vitality.

Our central interest lies with the effect of the Supreme Court's interpretation of precedent on the lower courts' usage of precedent, but we recognize the need to control for alternative explanations. We therefore include control variables utilized in prior chapters that capture two general factors: (1) particular characteristics of a precedent, such as the size of the coalition supporting it, which may influence its reach; and (2) factors that likely influence whether a precedent is cited or interpreted, either positively or negatively, by a court (e.g., *Breadth of Precedent*). These variables, and their respective measures, are discussed in chapter 4.[7]

We also control for several factors specific to the lower federal courts. First, we control for whether the precedent-setting case originated from a federal court of general jurisdiction. Presumably, the federal courts will be less likely to cite or interpret precedents resulting from cases originating in state courts or from federal courts of specialized jurisdiction. We include two dummy variables in our model: one designating whether the precedent-setting case originated in a federal court of *General Jurisdiction* and one noting whether the case originated in a federal court of *Specialized Jurisdiction*.[8] Cases originating in a state court serve as the baseline. Second, the number of cases decided by the lower federal courts has grown dramatically over the time period under study. As a result, it is likely that, as the caseload burgeons, federal courts have more opportunities to cite and interpret precedents. We control for this possibility by including a variable that records the number of cases, in 10,000's, filed in the U.S. Courts of Appeals and Federal District Courts each year (*Caseload*).[9]

Third, given that the policy preferences of federal judges influence their decisions (Goldman 1975; Rowland and Carp 1996; Songer, Sheehan, and Haire 2000), it is also likely that the manner in which the lower

[7] We do not include *Overruled Precedent* in these models because only two cases in this sample experienced this event. However, the results for *Precedent Vitality* are substantively the same if we include it.

[8] These data were taken from Spaeth (1995, 2001). Federal courts of general jurisdiction include all district courts, numbered circuit courts of appeals, and the DC Circuit Court of Appeals. During the time period of our analysis, federal courts of specialized jurisdiction include the Court of Customs and Patents Appeals, Court of International Trade, Court of Claims, Court of Federal Claims, Court of Military Appeals, Court of Appeals for the Armed Forces, Court of Military Review, Court of Veterans Appeals, Customs Court, Tax Court, and Court of Appeals for the Federal Circuit.

[9] We collected these data from the Administrative Office of the U.S. Courts (AO). The AO reports case filings from July 1 through June 30 of each year. For example, in 1990 the AO reports cases filed from July 1, 1989 through June 30, 1990. We therefore code the number of cases filed as the number listed in the report published that year.

federal courts use Supreme Court precedent is affected by the ideological compatibility between the judges on the lower courts and the Court precedent in question. We control for this effect by including *Lower Courts—Precedent Distance* in the models. For precedents established in cases in which the decision outcome was conservative, this variable equals the proportion of federal judges, in a given year, who were appointed by a Democratic president.[10] For liberal precedents, we measure *Lower Courts—Precedent Distance* as the proportion of federal judges, in a given year, who were appointed by a Republican president.

Finally, since our data contain multiple observations for each Court precedent, we need to control for the possibility that, despite all of our control variables, the residual for a precedent at time t will correlate with the residual at time $t - 1$. To account for serial correlation, we include the logged value of the lagged dependent variable in all three models (see Cameron and Trivedi 1998). In the citation model, for instance, we include the natural log of the number of citations at time $t - 1$ (i.e., the previous year) as an independent variable.[11] For all three models, we estimate robust standard errors that allow for correlation of errors within a precedent over time.[12]

Results

Given the large volume of cases decided in the lower federal courts, the rate of their interpretation of precedent is considerably higher than at the Supreme Court. The average annual number of lower court citations to a given Supreme Court precedent in our sample is 8.7. For positive and negative treatment, the average number of occurrences per year for a precedent is 0.9 and 0.4, respectively. These data indicate that while a

---

[10] The ideological direction of Supreme Court decisions is taken from Spaeth (1995, 2001). The data on partisan identification of the president who appointed judges sitting on the federal courts comes from the Federal Judicial Center's Federal Judges Biographical Database.

[11] To control for autocorrelation, Cameron and Trivedi (1998, 238, 295) recommend adding a constant (one that is greater than zero but less than one) to the lagged dependent variable, taking the log of the variable, and then including this variable as an independent variable. We therefore added 0.5 to the lagged dependent variable before taking its log. In addition, for the first year of the time series for a particular precedent (before which there can be no interpretations), the lagged dependent variable equals the natural log of 0.5. The results differ little if we instead use the untransformed lag of the dependent variable.

[12] In event count models, one issue of concern is the overabundance of zeros in the data, and one can account for such data with a zero-inflated count model. We estimated a zero-inflated negative binomial model with our data, and the results for *Precedent Vitality* are substantively the same as those presented here.

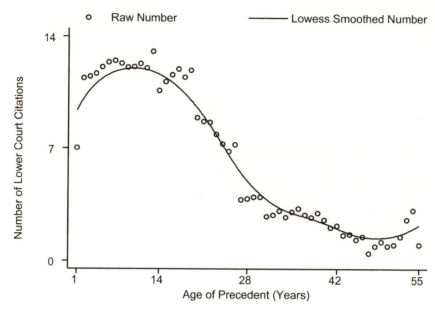

Figure 7.1. Average number of lower federal court citations of a Supreme Court precedent over time

Note: The authors collected these data from *Shepard's Citations.*

Supreme Court precedent is quite likely to be cited several times by the lower federal courts in a given year, precedents are not treated either positively or negatively at a particularly high rate. To provide further descriptive information about our dependent variables, figures 7.1 and 7.2 present plots of lower federal court usage of Court precedent over time. figure 7.1 depicts the rate at which lower courts cite the average precedent as it ages, while figure 7.2 presents a similar graph of the average number of positive and negative treatments of a precedent. For both figures, we present both the raw average rates of usage and smoothed plots of these rates.

These averages mask significant variation in the number of lower federal court interpretations and citations of a Supreme Court precedent in a year. The number of positive interpretations of a precedent in a year, for example, varies from 0 to 97, and the number of negative interpretations ranges from 0 to 26. As one would expect, there is even a wider variation for citations to precedent, with the number per year ranging from a low of 0 to a high of 504. It is these variations that we seek to explain.

Table 7.1 presents the results of our statistical analyses, which show that the U.S. Supreme Court's interpretation of a precedent influences how lower courts subsequently use it. Our data reveal that lower federal courts are more likely to cite or positively interpret precedents that are

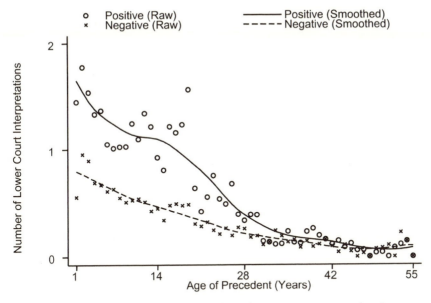

Figure 7.2. Average number of lower federal court treatments of a Supreme Court precedent over time

Note: The authors collected these data from *Shepard's Citations.*

more vital. This effect is evident in the positive and statistically significant coefficient estimates for *Precedent Vitality* in the citation and positive treatment models. The more that the Supreme Court has been interpreting a precedent in a positive manner, the more lower federal courts will follow and cite the precedent. The more that the Court interprets a precedent negatively, driving down its vitality, the less lower courts will follow and cite the precedent.

The estimate for *Precedent Vitality* in the negative interpretation model is in the predicted direction, negative, but is very small and not statistically significant. Thus, we cannot conclude that the Supreme Court's interpretation of precedent influences the extent to which the lower courts negatively treat the precedent. Taken together these results show that, at least for citation and positive interpretation, lower federal courts are responsive to the Supreme Court.

Substantively speaking, *Precedent Vitality* has a reasonably strong effect on lower court decisions. Figure 7.3 demonstrates this result by depicting the predicted number of citations as a function of the vitality of a precedent, while holding other variables constant.[13] If the Supreme Court

[13] We set all other independent variables at their means, except for dichotomous variables, which are set at their modes. *Precedent Vitality* ranges from the minimum to maximum values found in this sample of 200 Court precedents (−5 to 3).

TABLE 7.1

Negative Binomial Regression Models of Lower Federal Court Usage of Supreme Court Precedent

Independent Variable	Citations Coefficient (R.S.E.)	Positive Treatments Coefficient (R.S.E.)	Negative Treatments Coefficient (R.S.E.)
Precedent Vitality	.0726 (.0290)*	.0987 (.0556)*	−.0053 (.0505)
Control Variables:			
Vote Margin in Prec.	.0138 (.0129)	.0250 (.0215)	.0272 (.0211)
Conc. Opinions in Prec.	.1088 (.0676)	.1878 (.1283)	.1654 (.1160)
Total Prior Interp.'s	.1281 (.0203)*	.2031 (.0267)*	.1761 (.0336)*
Breadth of Precedent	−.1187 (.0673)	−.3714 (.1185)	−.2214 (.1204)
Amici Filings in Prec.	−.0777 (.0393)	−.0800 (.0682)	−.0674 (.0637)
Media Coverage of Prec.	.1456 (.0910)	.3713 (.1515)*	.4892 (.1563)*
Constitutional Prec.	.1377 (.0744)*	.0511 (.1148)	.0544 (.1069)
General Jurisdiction	.3124 (.0791)*	.3606 (.1403)*	.1145 (.1270)
Specialized Jurisdiction	−.1758 (.2592)	−2.050 (.3690)*	−1.987 (.3532)*
Age of Precedent	−.0836 (.0081)^	−.1022 (.0140)^	−.0795 (.0111)^
Age of Precedent Sq.	.0011 (.0001)^	.0009 (.0003)^	.0005 (.0002)^
Caseload	.0187 (.0033)*	.0463 (.0060)*	.0183 (.0050)*
Lower Courts—Precedent Distance	−.0029 (.1606)	.1484 (.2721)	−.0866 (.2578)
Per Curiam Precedent	−.5345 (.1899)*	−1.934 (.5931)*	−1.957 (.5401)*
Natural Log (y_{t-1})	.6954 (.0231)^	.8443 (.0457)^	.9134 (.0506)^
Constant	.4847 (.1408)^	−1.488 (.2635)^	−.8635 (.2093)^
α (dispersion parameter)	.4432*	.9352*	.7778*
Number of Observations	5,949	5,949	5,949
Log Likelihood	−13,688	−4763	−3869
Wald Test (Chi-square, 16 d.f.)	2628*	1276*	1270*

*p < .05 (one-tailed test); ^p <.05 (two-tailed test for non-directional controls and constants).

has positively interpreted a precedent and thus the precedent is vital, then the number of citations increases. For example, when a precedent has a low degree of vitality (*Precedent Vitality* = −5) then the lower courts cite it 2.3 times per year. Vital precedents (*Precedent Vitality* = 3) are cited at a rate of 4.1 times per year.

Our data show a similar effect on the positive usage of precedent. Before discussing the magnitude of this effect, we reiterate that positive in-

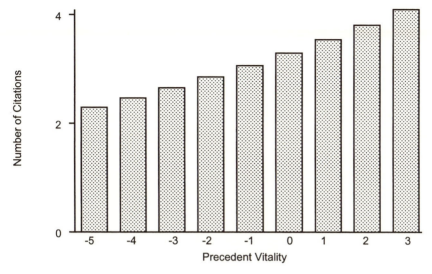

Figure 7.3. The influence of precedent vitality on lower federal courts' citation of Supreme Court precedent

Note: All other independent variables are set at their means, except for dichotomous variables, which are set at their modes.

terpretation occurs with less frequency than the citation of precedent. As figure 7.4 indicates, though, the number of positive interpretations does systematically fluctuate due to precedent vitality. The more densely shaded bars correspond to the predicted number of positive lower court treatments of an average Supreme Court precedent.[14] While the effect illustrated by these predictions is quite modest, the substantive effect of *Precedent Vitality* increases considerably when other variables increase the baseline number of positive interpretations accorded a precedent.[15] The less densely shaded bars depict the predicted number of positive treatments for a precedent that has an above-average baseline propensity for this type of treatment.[16] This second set of bars demonstrates the increasingly large effect of *Precedent Vitality* for precedents that are already somewhat more likely to be used in a positive manner in the lower courts.

[14] For the average precedent, we set all other independent variables at their means, except for dichotomous variables, which we set at their modal values.

[15] This is a function of the nonlinear nature of an event count model. As the dependent variable approaches zero, the effect size for any independent variable will be muted.

[16] For these predictions, we hold all the independent variables at the same values as for an average precedent, except for the natural log of the lagged dependent variable, which we set at two standard deviations above its mean.

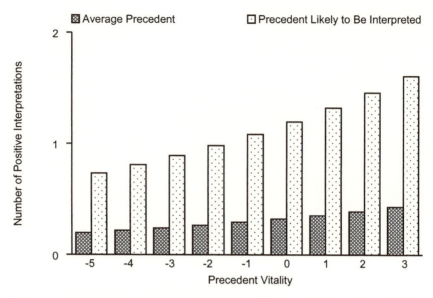

Figure 7.4. The influence of precedent vitality on lower federal courts' positive interpretation of Supreme Court precedent
Note: For the "Average precedent," all independent variables (except for *Precedent Vitality*) are set at their means/modes. For "precedent likely to be interpreted," the lagged dependent variable is set one standard deviation above its mean.

Our empirical models also include a series of control variables. First, we account for two variables—the size of the majority coalition in a precedent and the number of special concurring opinions accompanying a precedent—that prior research shows have some influence on the Supreme Court's interpretation of a precedent. Our results indicate that neither of these variables manifests any systematic influence on the lower courts' treatment of precedent.

Second, we include a set of variables tapping the extent to which a precedent is likely to be cited or interpreted. The total number of prior times the Supreme Court has interpreted a precedent increases lower federal courts' tendency to both cite and legally interpret it either positively or negatively. The two variables capturing the effect of precedent age indicate that as a case ages its usage decreases, and this negative effect flattens out as a case becomes quite old. For example, a one-half standard deviation increase in precedent age from below to above its mean (from 12 years old to 25 years old) moves the number of citations in a year from 3.8 to 2.1.[17] Also, lower federal courts are generally more likely to cite and interpret precedents set in cases that arrived at the Supreme Court from federal courts of general jurisdiction than cases originating from federal courts of specialized jurisdiction or state courts. The salience of a Court precedent (at the time it was established) has some effect, as cases reported on the front page of the *New York Times* when they were decided are more often interpreted positively or negatively. As we conjectured, the increase in the size of the federal judiciary's workload is positively correlated with citation and interpretation of precedent. Each of the lagged dependent variables is positive and statistically significant. The coefficient estimates for the rest of the control variables are statistically insignificant. It is particularly interesting that the ideological distance between the lower courts and the Supreme Court precedent appears to have no effect on how the lower courts use the precedent.[18]

The estimates for the alpha parameter are statistically significant in all three models. This result indicates that there is overdispersion in the data, meaning that the conditional variance is larger than the conditional mean. Thus, the negative binomial regression model is an appropriate choice over the more restrictive Poisson regression model, which assumes equidispersion of the data (Cameron and Trivedi 1998; Long 1997).

Finally, we consider several issues regarding the robustness of these results. First, we theoretically expect that it is appropriate to pool the data across the appellate courts and district courts in that vitality should exert the same effect at both levels of the judiciary.[19] We test this assumption by estimating our empirical model for appellate courts and district courts separately. The results are very similar to those we present in table 7.1. The only significant difference across the results is that the coefficient estimate for *Precedent Vitality* is not a statistically signif-

[17] Again, when generating these predicted event counts we set all other independent variables at their means/modes.

[18] One reason for why court ideology appears not to matter may be that our unit of analysis, the precedent-year, leads us to use an aggregate measure of ideology that does not capture variation across courts within a year. To more fully assess the role of ideology in this process, one would need to change the unit of analysis and include an observation for each precedent for each court for each year. Since our interest was to examine the influence of precedent vitality, we did not pursue that approach.

[19] It is not essential that we produce separate estimates for each court in our sample, as we do not theoretically expect there to be systematic differences across courts. In addition, the theoretical variable of interest, *Precedent Vitality*, does not vary across lower courts but only across time. Thus, for our purposes it would not be informative to differentiate across different courts. We note, however, that if one were principally interested in the influence of ideological distance between a court and a precedent, then such a strategy would be useful in that there would be variation across different courts at any single point in time.

icant predictor (although it is still in the predicted direction) of positive interpretations in the district courts.[20]

Second, we recognize that the use of *Shepard's* for lower courts may be somewhat more problematic than for the Supreme Court (Songer 1988; but see Benesh and Reddick 2002). For example, the distinguishing of a precedent by a lower court may be a more heterogeneous activity than at the Supreme Court, in large part because of the lower courts' lack of agenda control. A lower court opinion distinguishing a precedent put forward by an unsophisticated litigant in a case that has little overall meaning is not equivalent to the Supreme Court's decision to refuse to extend a case in a way that perhaps some lower courts had already done. One implication of this is that the lower courts' distinguishing of precedent may not be as responsive to precedent vitality as stronger forms of negative treatment. To test for this possibility, we estimated separate models for the lower federal courts' weak (Distinguished) and strong (Criticized, Limited, and Questioned) negative interpretation of precedent, finding that *Precedent Vitality* is negatively signed, but statistically insignificant, in both models.

CONCLUSION

The nature of a Supreme Court precedent can change over time as subsequent Court decisions shape the precedent by restricting or broadening its applicability. One of the assumptions that we make in this book is that the Supreme Court's interpretation of precedent represents a meaningful legal and political event that influences future outcomes. In this chapter, we directly test this assumption by examining the effect of the Court's interpretation of a precedent on how lower federal courts use the precedent.

Our analysis of more than 50 years of lower federal court usage of Supreme Court precedent demonstrates that precedent vitality, as defined by how the Court has treated or interpreted a case in the past, influences the number of times the courts cite or positively treat a Court precedent. These results indicate that the Supreme Court's treatment of its precedents matters because it has a real effect on how the lower courts then use the precedent. These data reinforce the argument we

---

[20] The coefficients (and standard errors) are .080 (.032) and .055 (.027), respectively, for appellate court and district court citation of precedent. For positive interpretation, the estimates are .130 (.065) and .071 (.059) for appellate and district courts, respectively. For negative interpretation, the estimates are −.026 (.064) and −.007 (.065), respectively, for appellate and district courts.

make earlier in this book that the Supreme Court's interpretation of precedent is a meaningful legal and political activity.

This is an important empirical result because it further substantiates our theoretical claim that there is an interactive relationship between the ideological distance between the justices and a precedent, and a precedent's legal vitality. The benefits the justices receive from moving policy closer to their preferred position, we have assumed, systematically differ depending on the precedent's legal vitality. A precedent's legal vitality affects how other decision makers use and interpret a precedent. By showing that lower court judges respond to legal vitality, we provide empirical support for this assumption.

A second implication that can be drawn from our analysis is that the Court's subsequent interpretation of a precedent exerts, for the most part, an effect on lower court usage of the precedent, while other factors that are often thought to determine the strength of a precedent do not exert the expected effect. Scholars suggest that the smaller the size of the coalition establishing the precedent (e.g., Benesh and Reddick 2002; Brenner and Spaeth 1995; Johnson 1987; Klein 2002; Pacelle and Baum 1992; Spriggs and Hansford 2001), the greater the number of separate opinions (e.g., Johnson 1987; Spriggs and Hansford 2001), and the older the precedent (Landes and Posner 1976), the less vital a precedent will be. Except for precedent age, it appears that lower court usage of Supreme Court precedent is not influenced much by these considerations, at least not in the expected manner. It appears that a common contention in the literature has no empirical support. Lower court usage of Court precedent (with the exception of negative treatment), however, does appear to be affected by how the Court has treated or interpreted the precedent. We can thus tentatively conclude that in the eyes of lower federal court judges, a Supreme Court precedent's vitality is more a function of subsequent Court interpretation of the precedent than most of these other possible indicators.

CHAPTER EIGHT

Concluding Remarks and Broader Implications

THE IMPORTANCE of the U.S. Supreme Court for American politics resides in its ability to set legal and public policy. The rules and procedures set forth in Court opinions serve important informational functions by helping to reduce uncertainty about the likely legal outcomes of the various courses of action that societal actors could undertake. Both governmental and nongovernmental decision makers can, for example, rely on Court precedent to decide whether to settle a lawsuit, set a workplace regulation, search or seize evidence, fire an employee, restrict an individual's ability to speak freely, or provide employment-related benefits. Simply put, Court opinions set precedents that affect the behavior of a wide range of actors.

Law is not a static concept but develops and changes over time. Almost everyone agrees that for the most part law develops incrementally based on judicial interpretations of it over time (e.g., Epstein and Knight 1998; Shapiro 1965). Alterations in the meaning and scope of law can have fundamental effects on resource allocations in society. While rule *A* at time *t* may, for instance, offer an advantage for labor versus business, a subsequent interpretation of that rule may shift this balance. By interpreting precedent, the Court determines opportunities in society and redistributes resources in both judicial and nonjudicial settings.

The importance of the Supreme Court's role in the development of the law raises an obvious yet important question: when, why, and how will the Court change the law? This question served as the motivation for this book. The specific aspect of legal change on which we chose to focus was the Court's positive and negative interpretation of the precedents it established in previous cases. The former occurs when the Court relies on a precedent when resolving a new dispute and in so doing reiterates its authority and possibly expands its scope. The latter takes place when the Court restricts the reach of a precedent or calls into question its continuing legal standing. By interpreting precedent as it decides disputes, the Court revisits legal principles and thus shapes the law.

SUMMARY OF THEORY AND RESULTS

We have contended that there are two motivations underpinning the Court's interpretation of precedent, both of which have to do with the justices' ultimate desire to influence societal outcomes in ways consistent with their preferences. The first motivation is to shape existing precedents so that they better reflect the preferences of the justices currently sitting on the Court. In order for Court policy to produce favorable outcomes it needs to be consistent with the justices' preferences. The second motivation behind the interpretation of precedent is to justify and promote the legitimacy of new policy choices contained in the Court's majority opinions. Since the Court is expected to provide legally relevant justifications for its decisions and cannot implement its own policy choices, the justices must rely in part on a decision's legitimacy to enhance the likelihood that other decision makers will implement or comply with it. By adhering to precedent, the Court can increase the extent to which its decisions are perceived as legitimate.

In chapter 2, we presented a theoretical model for the positive and negative interpretation of precedent based on these two motivations. We identified two variables driving the interpretation of precedent: the extent to which the justices agree with the policy content of a precedent and the legal vitality of a precedent. The former we conceptualized as the ideological incompatibility between the sitting justices on the Court and a precedent. We defined the latter as the legal reach and authority of a precedent as determined by the Court's prior interpretation of it. Our model also identified an important relationship between these two variables in which the influence of one depends on the state of the other.

Our theory yielded six propositions about how these variables influence when and how the Court will interpret or treat a precedent. We predicted that the justices will be more likely to positively interpret precedents with which they agree on policy grounds and less likely to negatively interpret such precedents. The model also hypothesized that increases in precedent vitality will raise the probability of positive interpretation for precedents that are ideologically distant from the Court. For precedents ideologically favored by the Court, precedents possessing greater vitality should be less likely to be negatively interpreted. With regard to the interactive effect between these two variables, precedent vitality should attenuate the negative effect of ideological distance on the probability of positive interpretation and enhance the positive effect of ideological distance on the likelihood of negative treatment. In other words, the degree to which a precedent is vital conditions the effect of the Supreme Court's ideological compatibility with the precedent on the Court's treatment of that precedent. Precedent vitality increases the importance of this ideological compatibility for the likelihood of the Court negatively interpreting a precedent, while decreasing the importance of this compatibility for the likelihood of positive interpretation.

We then empirically tested these propositions in chapters 4, 5, and 6.

Generally speaking, the data analyses provided convincing support for the predictions from our model. The results showed that the justices interpret precedent with a keen eye toward moving existing policy closer to their preferred policies. As the ideological distance between a precedent and the justices grows, for instance, we witnessed an increase in the likelihood of negative interpretation and a decrease in the occurrence of positive interpretation. The influence of the justices' policy goals also appeared in the conditioning effect that the vitality of a precedent exerted on the ideological distance between a precedent and the Court. Legally vital precedents are more likely to have broad social effects and thus these are precedents, for example, that an ideologically distant Court will attack.

We also demonstrated that the justices respond to the need to legitimize their policy choices with more legally authoritative cases. This effect is most apparent when considering that the justices may be more likely to positively interpret a precedent they ideologically favor if that precedent is particularly vital. This result, based on the logic presented in chapter 2, can only result from the justices' need to legitimize their policy choices.

Contrast the results for our hypotheses with the results for the alternative explanation that the type of treatment accorded a precedent will be a function of static precedent characteristics such as the relative size of the coalition that established the precedent. We find that coalition size and the presence of concurring opinions might increase the likelihood of a precedent being interpreted in the future, but these factors do not explain whether a precedent will be interpreted positively or whether it will be interpreted negatively. Consequently, the literature's long-standing contention that these characteristics of a precedent will influence a precedent's future usage appears largely unfounded. Likewise, precedent age affects whether, but not how, a precedent is interpreted. The variables central to our theoretical explanation, however, do provide leverage for explaining the type of interpretation given a precedent.

In addition, any study of the influence of precedent must confront the issue of endogeneity, or the possibility that the relationship between precedent and Court behavior is spurious. The basic premise of the norm of precedent is that prior actions of the Court are causally related to its present and future behavior. There is the possibility, however, that there are unobserved factors that caused legal treatment in the past, and thus influence our measure of *Precedent Vitality*, and continue to cause legal treatment in the future. It would then appear that *Precedent Vitality* is causing subsequent interpretations, while in fact it is the unobserved factors that drive both variables. The most likely unobserved factors that might operate here are any unmeasured ideological support that the Court has for the precedent and any unobserved static characteristics of a precedent regarding its "quality." It is thus important for us to show that *Precedent Vitality* is not simply capturing the extent to which the Court supports the precedent (to the extent that it is not already captured by our *Ideological Distance* variable and other control variables for the relevance or quality of a precedent).[1]

This endogeneity issue is an inherent obstacle to the study of the influence of precedent, but our model is not particularly susceptible to it. Importantly, a key element of our theoretical model—the interactive relationship between *Precedent Vitality* and *Ideological Distance*—is at odds with the endogeneity expectation. If *Precedent Vitality* simply captured any unmeasured support for the precedent, then there is no reason to expect that it would act to condition the effect of *Ideological Distance*. Rather, if *Precedent Vitality*'s effect is spurious, then it should be positively related to positive interpretation and negatively related to the negative interpretation of precedent, but vitality should not act to condition the effect of *Ideological Distance*. Simply put, if vitality just captures residual ideological distance or the quality of the precedent, then there is no reason why the effect of *Ideological Distance* would be conditional based on *Precedent Vitality*. Since our empirical analyses convincingly show that there is a conditional relationship between our two theoretical variables of interest, we conclude that the result for *Precedent Vitality* is real and not spurious.

Aside from the manner in which *Precedent Vitality* conditions the effect of *Ideological Distance*, the empirical results regarding the direct effect of *Precedent Vitality* on the interpretation of precedent are fully compatible with our predictions and are not entirely supportive of the endogeneity claim. We hypothesize that: (1) vitality will exert a positive effect on the probability of positive interpretation if the precedent is ideologically distant from the Court; and (2) vitality will exert a negative

---

[1] One might also suggest that our measure of *Precedent Vitality* could capture the unobserved relevance of a precedent. This is unlikely to be the case for two reasons. First, in our statistical models we control for the general relevance of the precedent with a large number of control variables. Second, if vitality is a surrogate for relevance, then vitality should not have a linear (or multiplicative) effect on the likelihood of positive or negative interpretation. Our measure of *Precedent Vitality* should not be acting as a surrogate for relevance, because either large positive values or large negative values would indicate that the precedent has been treated a number of times in the past. For prior interpretations to act as a surrogate for relevance, one would simply include a count of the total number of prior interpretations (where larger values would indicate a greater number of prior interpretations). This is precisely what we do when we include the *Total Prior Interpretations* control variable in our models. The inclusion of this control variable, along with the manner in which we measure vitality, allows us to be more confident that the measure of vitality is not tapping the general relevance of the precedent.

effect on the probability of negative interpretation if the precedent is ideologically close to the Court. Our theoretical model thus leads to predictions regarding the effect of vitality for certain ranges of ideological distance. For other ranges, our model does not predict an effect for vitality.

The data fully support our predictions. In chapter 4's positive interpretation model, for example, vitality exerts a positive and significant effect when ideological distance is high, while this effect is not significant when ideological distance is low. In the negative interpretation model of the same chapter, vitality exerts a negative and significant effect when ideological distance is low and a positive effect when ideological distance is high. These patterns in the data are fully consistent with our theoretical predictions.[2] The view of precedent vitality as spurious, however, would predict a somewhat different set of results. Under that account, the Court should *always* be more likely both to negatively interpret a precedent that has been treated negatively in the past and to positively interpret a precedent that has been interpreted positively in the past. Since the data fit our explanation better than this alternative one, we conclude that the vitality of a precedent plays a meaningful role in how the Court interprets it.

BROADER IMPLICATIONS

This book makes two specific contributions to the literature on law and legal change at the Supreme Court. First, it develops a new theoretical model of the interpretation of precedent. The model explains how the justices' policy goals and the legal vitality of precedent affect their decisions, and leads to precise predictions about when precedent will be interpreted positively or negatively. Our model suggests that the justices' ideological goals and the role of precedent are not mutually exclusive

---

[2] The same holds true in chapter 5; our prediction regarding vitality is fully supported, while the prediction drawn from the alternative explanation is only partly supported. In chapter 6, the results are somewhat mixed on this issue. For positive treatment, vitality exerts a positive effect regardless of ideological distance. This result is fully compatible with both our model and the alternative explanation. For negative treatment, the results conform to our expectations, while vitality's positive effect when *Ideological Distance* is high does not fit with the alternative explanation. In short, the empirical results for vitality are compatible with our expectations for all five statistical models. The results are fully compatible with the alternative explanation's argument in one out of the five. For the other four models, the results are only compatible with the alternative explanation when *Ideological Distance* is limited to a specific range of values. We take all of this as evidence that *Precedent Vitality* is largely operating as we anticipated. It is not simply tapping whether the precedent is supported by the Court or not.

considerations, as is often argued in the literature. Rather, each of these factors is important as the justices attempt to set policy that reflects their preferences and encourages the downstream societal effects they desire.

The second contribution comes from the empirical tests of our model. We present a series of rigorous, quantitative tests of our hypotheses that demonstrate their explanatory power. By examining the Court's treatment of all its precedents decided from the 1946 through 1999 terms, we provide the broadest empirical analysis of the interpretation of precedent to date. Taken together, our theory and data provide a more refined understanding of legal development at the Court.

Beyond these specific additions to the literature, our study points to several more general conclusions or implications. The first lesson drawn from our analysis is that the policy preferences of the justices not only affect their votes on the merits of a case (see Segal and Spaeth 2002), they also influence how the Court handles existing precedents when deciding a case. Precedents that conflict with a Court's preferences are less likely to be interpreted in a positive manner and are more likely to be distinguished, limited, or even overruled. The importance of judicial preferences to the body of extant precedent further reinforces the importance of nominations to the Supreme Court. The changes in Supreme Court preferences that can result from the arrival of new justices have real implications for the future meaning and authority of precedents set by prior Courts.

A second implication pertains to what is currently one of the most heated debates among judicial experts: Does precedent influence Supreme Court decision making? Generally speaking, the literature tends to present two seemingly incompatible visions of judging. Scholars from the attitudinal school of thought contend that precedent has *no* systematic influence on the policy choices made by the justices. According to this model's main proponents, "precedent as a component of the legal model provides virtually no guide to the justices' decisions" (Segal and Spaeth 2002, 81). Other scholars, by contrast, either argue that precedent is a central, if not controlling, variable in decision making (e.g., Dworkin 1978; Kahn 1999) or at least posit that precedent constrains the justices' decisions (e.g., Knight and Epstein 1996; Wahlbeck 1997). While many scholars recognize that both of these variables may matter (e.g., Baum 1997; McGuire and MacKuen 2001), much of the literature continues to present them as competing explanations (e.g., George and Epstein 1992; Segal and Spaeth 2002).

Our study suggests that this tendency in the literature misses an essential element of Supreme Court decision making. Law and policy are not irreconcilable features of the judicial arena; they are both important considerations that are inextricably linked to one another as the justices interpret and shape the law. While precedent can operate as a constraint on the justices' decisions, it also represents an opportunity. It can be a constraint in that, under certain circumstances, the justices will respond to the need to legitimize their policy choices, and this incentive affects how they use precedent. It can represent an opportunity in that it is through the setting and interpreting of precedent that the justices can foster outcomes in society that they prefer. The main point is that the justices do not change law simply based on their policy preferences or on the existing state of precedent; they do so based on an interactive relationship between these two factors.

A third inference we draw from our study pertains to the two motivations underlying the interpretation of precedent. We have argued that the justices interpret precedent in order to move existing precedents closer to their preferred outcomes and to justify new policy choices. While we had specific expectations regarding the manner in which precedent vitality conditions the effect of the ideological distance between the Court and a precedent, the direct effect of precedent vitality on either the positive or negative interpretation of precedent depends on which of these two motivations is more important. While our theory was agnostic as to which of these two incentives held greater sway over the justices, our data allow us to comment on their relative significance. Overall, our data show that both the justices' desire to set policy consistent with their preferences and their need to justify their new policies influence their decisions. With regard to the positive interpretation of precedent, we find that the legitimacy incentive may be of somewhat greater importance than the desire to alter extant precedent. When turning to negative interpretation, however, we see that the justices' desire to diminish the authority of cases with which they ideologically disagree tends to play a bigger role than the potential legitimacy loss associated with negatively treating precedents that are more vital.

What does this particular empirical result tell us about Supreme Court decision making? Perhaps the following or positive treatment of precedent is fundamentally, though not solely, more of a legitimizing activity, while the negative treatment of precedent is more of an exercise in molding precedent to fit the justices' policy preferences. After all, the norm of *stare decisis* requires the former behavior, but not the latter. This is *not* to say, for example, that the positive interpretation of precedent is solely a function of legitimacy concerns. It just appears that legitimacy concerns may do more to drive the positive interpretation than the desire to shape extant precedent in a favorable manner.

This might explain why we find that the lower courts' positive usage of Supreme Court precedent is affected by the vitality of the precedent but their negative usage of precedent is not. When examining how the lower courts use Court precedent, we implicitly focused on the legitimacy motivation. That is, we expected precedent vitality to have a simple additive effect on how the lower courts use a Supreme Court precedent. The more vital a precedent is, the more likely the lower courts are to cite and follow it. The less vital a precedent, the more likely the lower courts are to use it in a negative fashion. We find that the former pair of relationships exists but the latter does not. If the positive interpretation of precedent is more an exercise in the legitimization of decisions, then it makes sense that lower courts would be particularly responsive to the vitality of a precedent when deciding whether to follow it. If lower courts are relatively unconcerned with the legitimacy costs associated with treating a Supreme Court precedent negatively, then we should see precedent vitality not playing much of a role in the decision to use a precedent negatively, at least not in a simple additive manner. In short, the results of all our empirical chapters point to the conclusion that when treating a precedent positively the justices are more motivated by legitimacy concerns, while when treating a precedent negatively they are primarily motivated by the desire to shape extant legal policy.

Fourth, it is important for us to point out that this study has clear implications for all scholars studying law and legal change, not just those doing so as political scientists. Sociologists, economists, and law professors often endeavor to understand how the Court crafts law. But, with few exceptions (e.g., Landes and Posner 1976; Phillips and Grattet 2000), they have not produced empirically falsifiable hypotheses that explain legal change. Consider, for instance, the school of thought known as Critical Legal Studies (CLS). The origins of this movement can be traced to Legal Realism, which holds that judges make decisions based on their ideological leanings or sense of fairness, in light of the facts of a case (see Leiter 1997; Segal and Spaeth 2002). Critical Legal Studies is a neo-Marxian offshoot of Legal Realism that criticizes law as preserving illegitimate power relationships in society (see Tushnet 1988; Unger 1983). Scholars working in this tradition further emphasize the role of ideology in shaping the law and argue that since law is indeterminate (i.e., it does not lead to particular outcomes) judges can justify any policy they desire. In effect, CLS denies that legal reasoning, precedent, and *stare decisis* have any causal force in judicial decision making.

It should be obvious by now that our theory and data point to a decidedly different conclusion about the role of law than that drawn by Critical Legal Studies. While judges most certainly pursue their policy preferences, we argue and empirically demonstrate that, at times, they also respond to the need to legitimize their policy choices. Judges possess discretion, but it is not limitless because they must provide legally reasoned decisions in order to legitimize their policy choices. Most notably, we show that an element of *stare decisis*, the vitality of a precedent, influences the way in which justices on the U.S. Supreme Court interpret precedent.

Finally, this study reinforces an important point that scholars of judicial politics have recently been making: "explorations of the Supreme Court should not begin and end with examinations of the vote, as they have for so many years. Rather, we must explore the range of choices that contribute to the development of law" (Epstein and Knight 1998, 185). Our study demonstrates that by examining dependent variables regarding law and legal change, we gain new insight into the fundamentals of Court decision making.

A focus on legal development, for example, helps to bridge the decades-old debate between legalists and attitudinalists. While some may contend (rightly) that these two models, as models, represent straw men, recent notable publications (e.g., Clayton and Gillman 1999; Segal and Spaeth 2002; Spaeth and Segal 1999), and critical responses to that research (Gillman 2003; Kritzer 2003; Segal and Spaeth 2003; Spriggs 2003) show that both are alive and kicking (some might even say screaming). Quite simply, we show that an explanation of legal change requires us to go beyond the traditional boundaries drawn by these competing accounts. A pure focus on the justices' policy preferences or a sole focus on legal considerations cannot explain legal change. By taking essential features of both of these perspectives and building them into a model of legal interpretation, however, we are better able to understand legal change at the Court.

CONCLUSION

Our goal was an ambitious one: to explain legal development at the U.S. Supreme Court. The extent to which we have done so, of course, will be determined by the reader. We have sought to produce an analysis that, as much as possible, satisfies the two dominant goals of social science: the development of parsimonious theory and the systematic empirical testing of it. We must, however, reiterate several caveats discussed at various point in this book about the scope of our analysis and the conclusions we can derive from it.

The first point is that this book most certainly does not exhaust the study of legal change at the Court. The scope of the analysis in this book, while broad in some respects, is narrow in others. Most notably, our choice to focus on the interpretation of precedent, while revealing an important part of Court decision making, does not capture the full range of the way in which law changes at the Court. Future studies thus have much room to develop additional dependent variables that represent how law develops over time and within cases.

We also deliberately created a theoretical framework that was parsimonious and centered on what we see as the two primary variables behind legal change. While this choice results in a tightly focused explanation and clear predictions, it does downplay variables that some might see as being relevant. Our empirical models attempted to control for as many of these alternative explanations as possible, and future research may uncover additional factors that are relevant. In addition, our theory is about the U.S. Supreme Court, and we hope that future studies will adapt and modify our framework and apply it to lower courts.

A third caveat follows from our choice to utilize a quantitative approach to test our hypotheses. The research designs we employ allow us to draw generalizable inferences, but do not provide the descriptive richness of a more qualitative approach. We have, however, attempted to provide substantive examples and qualitative illustrations where possible.

Fourth, the theoretical concepts central to our explanation are difficult to measure. We have taken advantage of what we view as the most appropriate data available for capturing the preferences of the justices, the ideological content of precedent, and the legal vitality of precedent. Naturally, the proxies we use for these variables are not perfect, and our hope is that future research will develop more refined measures of them that may further reveal nuances in how law develops.

We end this book where we began it, with the recognition that Supreme Court decisions contain public policies that can fundamentally affect the allocation of resources in society. This is precisely why we find the Court an interesting decision-making body to study. In the preceding pages, we have attempted to explain when and why one aspect of these policies, the meaning of precedent, changes. We think readers will know more about legal development at the Court after reading this book, but we recognize, and hope, that future treatments of it will further enhance our understanding. In this sense, our study shares a common feature with legal change in that it represents an incremental step in an ongoing quest to answer important questions.

Appendix

Table A.1
Summary Statistics for Independent Variables Used in Chapter 4

Independent Variable	Mean	Standard Deviation	Minimum	Maximum
Ideological Distance (*ID*)	10.80	10.63	0	52.3
Precedent Vitality (*V*)	−.08	.98	−8	17
Ideological Distance × Vitality (*ID × V*)	−1.77	18.72	−311.2	304.15
Concurring Opinions in Precedent	.22	.53	0	5
Voting Margin in Precedent	5.33	2.95	0	9
Total Prior Interpretations	1.02	1.91	0	41
Court Agenda	17.20	10.08	0	47
Breadth of Precedent	0	.44	−.53	4.44
Amici Filings	.01	1.0	−1.10	9.99
Media Coverage	.15	.35	0	1
Per Curiam Precedent	.09	.29	0	1
Constitutional Precedent	.33	.47	0	1
Overruled Precedent	.01	.11	0	1
Age of Precedent	18.57	12.87	1	56
Age of Precedent Squared	510.53	608.41	1	3,136

TABLE A.2
Summary Statistics for Independent Variables Used in Chapter 5

Independent Variable	Mean	Standard Deviation	Minimum	Maximum
Ideological Distance (*ID*)	10.77	10.61	0	52.3
Precedent Vitality (*V*)	−.06	.95	−7	17
Ideological Distance × Vitality (*ID* × *V*)	−1.51	18.06	−272.3	304.15
Concurring Opinions in Precedent	.22	.53	0	5
Voting Margin in Precedent	5.35	2.95	0	9
Total Prior Interpretations	.99	1.87	0	41
Court Agenda	17.15	10.08	0	47
Breadth of Precedent	−.003	.44	−.53	4.44
Amici Filings	.007	1.0	−1.10	9.99
Media Coverage	.15	.35	0	1
Per Curiam Precedent	.09	.29	0	1
Constitutional Precedent	.33	.47	0	1

TABLE A.3
Summary Statistics for Independent Variables Used in Chapter 6

Independent Variable	Mean	Standard Deviation	Minimum	Maximum
Ideological Distance (*ID*)	17.35	12.64	0	74.4
Precedent Vitality (*V*)	−.04	1.17	−8	16
Ideological Distance × Vitality (*ID*×*V*)	−1.59	27.54	−472	572.8
Concurring Opinions in Precedent	.26	.57	0	5
Voting Margin in Precedent	5.35	2.99	0	9
Total Prior Interpretations	1.40	2.34	0	40
Breadth of Precedent	−.003	.43	−.53	4.44
Amici Filings in Precedent	.01	1.0	−1.10	9.99
Media Coverage of Precedent	.15	.36	0	1
Per Curiam Precedent	.08	.27	0	1
Constitutional Precedent	.35	.48	0	1
Overruled Precedent	.02	.13	0	1
Age of Precedent	24.76	13.93	1	55
Age of Precedent Squared	807.13	750.21	1	3025
Number of Citing Briefs	.02	.26	0	29
Same Broad Issue	.16	.37	0	1
Same Narrow Issue	.01	.11	0	1
Same Legal Provision	.03	.16	0	1
Same Authority	.30	.46	0	1
Amici Filings in Treatment Case	.23	1.19	−.85	6.28
Breadth of Treatment Case	−.04	.34	−.53	1.47
Number of Precedents Cited in Briefs	134.55	119.43	8	813

TABLE A.4
Summary Statistics for Independent Variables Used in Chapter 7

Independent Variable	Mean	Standard Deviation	Minimum	Maximum
Precedent Vitality	−.22	.96	−5	3
Vote Margin in Precedent	5.12	2.89	0	9
Conc. Opinions in Precedent	.17	.39	0	2
Total Prior Interpretations	1.03	1.66	0	13
Breadth of Precedent	.03	.45	−.54	1.57
Amici Filings in Precedent	−.01	.94	−1.02	5.37
Media Coverage of Precedent	.12	.33	0	1
Constitutional Precedent	.32	.47	0	1
General Jurisdiction	.75	.43	0	1
Specialized Jurisdiction	.01	.10	0	1
Age of Precedent	18.73	12.92	1	55
Age of Precedent Squared	517.69	610.47	1	3025
Caseload	26.37	9.94	8.16	37.70
Lower Courts— Precedent Distance	.49	.13	.16	.84
Per Curiam Precedent	.09	.29	0	1
Natural Log (neutral t_{-1})	1.01	1.42	−.69	6.22
Natural Log (positive t_{-1})	−.30	.78	−.69	4.18
Natural Log (negative t_{-1})	−.39	.62	−.69	3.28

References

Aero Mayflower Transit Co. v. Board of Railroad Commissioners. 1947. 332 U.S. 495.

Aguilar v. Texas. 1964. 378 U.S. 108.

Aldisert, Rugero J. 1990. "Precedent: What It Is and What It Isn't; When Do We Kiss It and When Do We Kill It?" *Pepperdine Law Review* 17(April):605–36.

Allen, Carleton Kemp. 1964. *Law in the Making.* 7th ed. New York: Clarendon Press.

Amalgamated Food Employees Union Local 590 v. Logan Valley Plaza, Inc. 1968. 391 U.S. 308.

American Insurance Association v. Garamendi. 2003. 156 L.Ed. 2d 376.

American Trucking Assns., Inc. v. Scheiner. 1987. 483 U.S. 266.

Anders v. California. 1967. 386 U.S. 738.

AT&T Technologies v. Communications Workers of America. 1986. 475 U.S. 643.

Banks, Christopher P. 1992. "The Supreme Court and Precedent: An Analysis of Natural Courts and Reversal Trends." *Judicature* 75(February–March): 262–68.

Baum, Lawrence. 1988. "Measuring Policy Change in the U.S. Supreme Court." *American Political Science Review* 82(September):905–12.

———. 1997. *The Puzzle of Judicial Behavior.* Ann Arbor: University of Michigan Press.

———. 2001. *The Supreme Court.* 7th ed. Washington, DC: Congressional Quarterly Press.

Beck, Nathaniel, Jonathan N. Katz, and Richard Tucker. 1998. "Taking Time Seriously: Time Series-Cross Section Analysis with a Binary Dependent Variable." *American Journal of Political Science* 42(October):1260–88.

Benesh, Sara C. 2002. *The U.S. Courts of Appeals and the Law of Confessions: Perspectives on the Hierarchy of Justice.* New York: LFP Scholarly Publishing.

Benesh, Sara, and Malia Reddick. 2002. "Overruled: An Event History Analysis of Lower Court Reaction to Supreme Court Alteration of Precedent." *Journal of Politics* 64(May):534–50.

Bhala, Raj. 1999. "The Precedent Setters: *De Facto Stare Decisis* in WTO Adjudication." *Journal of Transnational Law & Policy* 9(Fall):1–151.

Bond, Jon R., and Charles A. Johnson. 1982. "Implementing a Permissive Policy: Hospital Abortion Services after *Roe v. Wade.*" *American Journal of Political Science* 26(February):1–24.

Boucher, Robert L., and Jeffrey A. Segal. 1995. "Supreme Court Justices as Strategic Decision Makers: Aggressive Grants and Defensive Denials on the Vinson Court." *Journal of Politics* 57(August):824–37.

Box-Steffensmeier, Janet M., and Bradford S. Jones. 2004. *Event History Modeling: A Guide for Social Scientists.* Cambridge: Cambridge University Press.

Brenner, Saul. 1982. "Strategic Choice and Opinion Assignment on the U.S. Supreme Court: A Reexamination." *Western Political Quarterly* 35(June): 204–11.

Brenner, Saul, and Harold J. Spaeth. 1988. "Ideological Position as a Variable in the Authoring of Dissenting Opinions on the Warren and Burger Courts." *American Politics Quarterly* 16(July):317–28.

———. 1995. *Stare Indecisis: The Alteration of Precedent on the U.S. Supreme Court, 1946–1992*. New York: Cambridge University Press.

Brenner, Saul, and Marc Stier. 1996. "Retesting Segal and Spaeth's *Stare Decisis* Model." *American Journal of Political Science* 40(November):1036–48.

Bueno de Mesquita, Ethan, and Matthew Stephenson. 2002. "Informative Precedent and Intrajudicial Communication." *American Political Science Review* 96(December):755–66.

Bush v. Gore. 2000. 531 U.S. 98.

Bush v. Vera. 1996. 517. U.S. 952.

Caldeira, Gregory A. 1985. "The Transmission of Legal Precedent: A Study of State Supreme Courts." *American Political Science Review* 79(March): 178–93.

———. 1986. "Neither the Purse Nor the Sword: Dynamics of Public Confidence in the Supreme Court." *American Political Science Review* 80(December):1209–26.

———. 1988. "Legal Precedent: Structures of Communication between State Supreme Courts." *Social Networks* 10(March):29–55.

Caldeira, Gregory A., John R. Wright, and Christoper J. W. Zorn. 1999. "Strategic Voting and Gatekeeping in the Supreme Court." *Journal of Law, Economics, & Organization* 15(October):549–72.

Cameron, Charles M., Jeffrey A. Segal, and Donald Songer. 2000. "Strategic Auditing in a Political Hierarchy: An Informational Model of the Supreme Court's Certiorari Decisions." *American Political Science Review* 94(March): 101–16.

Cameron, A. Colin, and Pravin K. Trivedi. 1998. *Regression Analysis of Count Data*. New York: Cambridge University Press.

Canon, Bradley C. 1973. "Reactions of State Supreme Courts to a U.S. Supreme Court Civil Liberties Decision." *Law & Society Review* 8(Fall):109–34.

———. 1977. "Testing the Effectiveness of Civil Liberties Policies at the State and Federal Levels: The Case of the Exclusionary Rule." *American Politics Quarterly* 5(January):57–82.

Canon, Bradley C., and Charles A. Johnson. 1999. *Judicial Policies: Implementation and Impact*. 2nd ed. Washington, DC: Congressional Quarterly Press.

Cardozo, Benjamin. [1921] 1964. *The Nature of the Judicial Process*. New Haven, CT: Yale University Press.

Carmines, Edward G., and Richard A. Zeller. 1979. *Reliability and Validity Assessment*. Newbury Park, CA: SAGE Publications.

Carter, Leif. 1988. *Reason in Law*. 4th ed. New York: Harper Collins.

Central Hardware Co. v. National Labor Relations Board. 1972. 407 U.S. 539.

Circuit City Stores v. Adams. 2001. 532 U.S. 105.

Clayton, Cornell W., and Howard Gillman, eds. 1999. *Supreme Court Decision-Making: New Institutionalist Approaches*. Chicago: University of Chicago Press.

Cohen, Jacob. 1960. "A Coefficient of Agreement for Nominal Scales." *Education and Psychological Measurement* 20(1):37–46.

Comparato, Scott A., and Scott D. McClurg. 2003. "Ambiguity in the Transmission of Precedent: A Team Theoretic Approach to the Relationship between the Supreme Court and State Supreme Courts." Presented at the Annual Meeting of the American Political Science Association, Philadelphia, PA, August 28–31.

Cooter, Robert, Stephen Marks, and Robert Mnookin. 1982. "Bargaining in the Shadow of the Law." *Journal of Legal Studies* 11(June):225–51.

Danelski, David J. 1986. "Causes and Consequences of Conflict and Its Resolution in Supreme Court." In *Judicial Conflict and Consensus: Behavioral Studies of American Appellate Courts*, ed. Charles M. Lamb and Sheldon Goldman. Lexington, KY: University Press of Kentucky.

DeJonge v. Oregon. 1937. 229 U.S. 353.

Department of Taxation and Finance of New York v. Milhelm Attea and Bros. 1994. 512 U.S. 61.

Dometrius, Nelson C., and Lee Sigelman. 1988. "Modeling the Impact of Supreme Court Decisions." *Journal of Politics* 50(February):131–49.

Douglas, William O. [1949] 1979. "Stare Decisis." In *Courts, Judges, and Politics: An Introduction to the Judicial Process*, ed. Walter F. Murphy and C. Herman Pritchett. New York: Random House.

Dworkin, Ronald. 1978. *Taking Rights Seriously*. Cambridge, MA: Harvard University Press.

Epstein, Lee, and Gary King. 2002. "The Rules of Inference." *University of Chicago Law Review* 69(Winter):1–133.

Epstein, Lee, and Jack Knight. 1998. *The Choices Justices Make*. Washington, DC: Congressional Quarterly Press.

Epstein, Lee, and Joseph F. Kobylka. 1992. *The Supreme Court and Legal Change: Abortion and the Death Penalty*. Chapel Hill, NC: University of North Carolina Press.

Epstein, Lee, and Carol Mershon. 1996. "Measuring Political Preferences." *American Journal of Political Science* 40(February):261–94.

Epstein, Lee, and Jeffrey A. Segal. 2000. "Measuring Issue Salience." *American Journal of Political Science* 44(January):66–85.

Epstein, Lee, Jeffrey A. Segal, and Timothy Johnson. 1996. "The Claim of Issue Creation on the U.S. Supreme Court." *American Political Science Review* 90(December):845–52.

Epstein, Lee, Jeffrey A. Segal, and Harold J. Spaeth. 2001. "The Norm of Consensus on the U.S. Supreme Court." *American Journal of Political Science* 45(April):362–77.

Epstein, Lee, Jeffrey A. Segal, Harold J. Spaeth, and Thomas G. Walker. 1996. *The Supreme Court Compendium: Data, Decisions and Developments*. Washington, DC: Congressional Quarterly Press.

Eskridge, William N., Jr. 1991. "Overriding Supreme Court Statutory Interpretation Decisions." *Yale Law Journal* 101(November):331–455.

Estelle v. McGuire. 1991. 502 U.S. 62.

Fenno, Richard F. 1986. "Observation, Context, and Sequence in the Study of Politics." *American Political Science Review* 80(March):3–15.

Flemming, Roy B., John Bohte, and B. Dan Wood. 1997. "One Voice among Many: The Supreme Court's Influence on Attentiveness to Issues in the United States, 1947–92." *American Journal of Political Science* 41(October): 1224–50.

Freed, Todd E. 1996. "Is Stare Decisis Still the Lighthouse Beacon of Supreme Court Jurisprudence? A Critical Analysis." *Ohio State Law Journal* 57(5): 1767–97.

Friedman, Lawrence M. 1985. *A History of American Law*. 2nd ed. New York: Simon and Schuster.

Friedman, Lawrence M., Robert A. Kagan, Bliss Cartwright, and Stanton Wheeler. 1981. "State Supreme Courts: A Century of Style and Citation." *Stanford Law Review* 33(May):773–818.

Friedrich, Robert J. 1982. "In Defense of Multiplicative Terms in Multiple Regression Equations." *American Journal of Political Science* 26(November): 797–833.

Gates, John B., and Glenn A. Phelps. 1996. "Intentionalism in Constitutional Opinions." *Political Research Quarterly* 48(June):245–61.

Gely, Rafael, and Pablo T. Spiller. 1992. "The Political Economy of Supreme Court Constitutional Decisions: The Case of Roosevelt's Court-Packing Plan." *International Review of Law and Economics* 12(March):45–67.

George, Tracey E., and Lee Epstein. 1992. "On the Nature of Supreme Court Decision Making." *American Political Science Review* 86(June):323–37.

Gerhardt, Michael J. 1991. "The Role of Precedent in Constitutional Decisionmaking and Theory." *George Washington Law Review* 60(November): 68–159.

Gibson, James, L. 1989. "Understandings of Justice: Institutional Legitimacy, Procedural Justice, and Political Tolerance." *Law & Society Review* 23(3): 469–96.

———. 1997. United States Supreme Court Judicial Database, Phase II: 1953–1993 (Study #6987). ICPSR version. Houston, TX: University of Houston [producer], 1996. Ann Arbor, MI: Inter-university Consortium for Political and Social Research [distributor], 1997.

Gibson, James L., and Gregory A. Caldeira. 1992. "The Etiology of Public Support for the Supreme Court." *American Journal of Political Science* 36 (August):635–64.

Gibson, James L., Gregory A. Caldeira, and Vanessa A. Baird. 1998. "On the Legitimacy of National High Courts." *American Political Science Review* 92(June):343–58.

Gill, Jeff. n.d. "Interactions in Generalized Linear Models: Theoretical Issues and an Application to Judicial Decision Making." University of California, Davis. Typescript.

Gillman, Howard. 1993. *The Constitution Besieged: The Rise and Demise of Lochner Era Police Powers Jurisprudence*. Durham, NC: Duke University Press.

———. 1999. "The Court as an Idea, Not a Building (or a Game): Interpretive Institutionalism and the Analysis of Supreme Court Decision-Making." In *Supreme Court Decision-Making: New Institutionalist Approaches*, ed. Cornell W. Clayton and Howard Gillman. Chicago: University of Chicago Press.

———. 2003. "Separating the Wheat from the Chaff in *The Supreme Court and the Attitudinal Model Revisited.*" *Law and Courts Newsletter* 13(Summer): 12–18.

Ginsburg, Ruth Bader. 1990. "Remarks on Writing Separately." *Washington Law Review* 65(January):133–50.

———. 1995. "Communicating and Commenting on the Court's Work." *Georgetown Law Journal* 83(July):2119–28.

———. 2004. "Speaking in a Judicial Voice: Reflections on *Roe v. Wade.*" In *Judges on Judging: Views from the Bench*. 2nd ed. Ed. David M. O'Brien. Washington, DC: Congressional Quarterly Press.

Gitlow v. New York. 1925. 268 U.S. 652.

Glick, James. 1994. "The Impact of Permissive Judicial Policies: The U.S. Supreme Court and the Right to Die." *Political Research Quarterly* 47(March): 207–22.

Goldman, Sheldon. 1975. "Voting Behavior on the United States Courts of Appeals, Revisited." *American Political Science Review* 69(June):491–506.

Grady v. Corbin. 1990. 495 U.S. 508.

Green Tree Financial Corp. v. Bazzle. 2003. 156 L.Ed. 2d 414.

Greene, William H. 1997. *Econometric Analysis*. 3rd ed. Upper Saddle River, NJ: Prentice Hall.

Greenhouse, Linda. 2000. "Another Kind of Bitter Split." *The New York Times*, Dec. 14:A1.

Grosskopf, Anke, and Jeffery J. Mondak. 1998. "Do Attitudes toward Specific Supreme Court Decisions Matter? The Impact of *Webster* and *Texas v. Johnson* on Public Confidence in the Supreme Court." *Political Research Quarterly* 51(September):633–54.

Grutter v. Bollinger. 2003. 156 L.Ed. 2d 304.

Harris v. United States. 2002. 536 U.S. 545.

Harris, Peter. 1985. "Ecology and Culture in the Communication of Precedent among State Supreme Courts, 1870–1970." *Law & Society Review* 19(3): 449–86.

Hoekstra, Valerie J. 2000. "The Supreme Court and Local Public Opinion." *American Political Science Review* 94(March):89–100.

———. 2003. *Public Reactions to Supreme Court Decisions*. New York: Cambridge University Press.

Hubbard v. United States. 1995. 514 U.S. 695.

Hudgens v. National Labor Relations Board. 1976. 424 U.S. 507.

Illinois v. Gates. 1983. 462 U.S. 213.

Johnson, Charles A. 1979. "Lower Court Reactions to Supreme Court Decisions: A Quantitative Examination." *American Journal of Political Science* 23(November):792–804.

———. 1985. "Citations to Authority in Supreme Court Opinions." *Law and Policy* 7(October):509–23.

———. 1986. "Follow-Up Citations in the U.S. Supreme Court." *Western Political Quarterly* 39(September):538–47.

———. 1987. "Law, Politics, and Judicial Decision Making: Lower Federal Court Uses of Supreme Court Decisions." *Law & Society Review* 21(2): 325–40.

Johnson, Charles A., and Bradley C. Canon. 1984. *Judicial Policies: Implementation and Impact*. Washington, DC: Congressional Quarterly Press.

Johnson, Timothy R. 2004. *Oral Arguments and Decision Making on the United States Supreme Court*. Albany: State University of New York Press.

Johnson, Timothy R., and Andrew Martin. 1998. "The Public's Conditional Response to Supreme Court Decisions." *American Political Science Review* 92(June): 299–327.

Kahn, Ronald. 1999. "Institutional Norms and Supreme Court Decision Making: The Rehnquist Court on Privacy and Religion." In *Supreme Court Decision-Making: New Institutionalist Approaches*, ed. Cornell W. Clayton and Howard Gillman. Chicago: University of Chicago Press.

Kempin, Frederick G., Jr. 1959. "Precedent and Stare Decisis: The Critical Years, 1800 to 1850." *The American Journal of Legal History* 3(January):28–54.

King, Gary, Robert O. Keohane, and Sidney Verba. 1994. *Designing Social Inquiry*. Princeton, NJ: Princeton University Press.

King, Gary, and Langche Zeng. 2001. "Logistic Regression in Rare Events Data." *Political Analysis* 9(Spring):137–63.

Klein, David E. 2002. *Making Law in the United States Courts of Appeals*. New York: Cambridge University Press.

Klein, David E., and Robert Hume. 2003. "Fear of Reversal as an Explanation of Lower Court Compliance." *Law & Society Review* 37(September): 579–606.

Knight, Jack, and Lee Epstein. 1996. "The Norm of *Stare Decisis*." *American Journal of Political Science* 40(November):1018–35.

Kosma, Montgomery N. 1998. "Measuring the Influence of Supreme Court Justices." *Journal of Legal Studies* 27(June):333–72.

Krippendorf, Klaus. 1980. *Content Analysis: An Introduction to Its Methodology*. Beverly Hills, CA: SAGE Publications.

Kritzer, Herbert M. 2003. "Have Segal and Spaeth Finally Driven a Stake through the Heart of the Legal Model?" *Law and Courts Newsletter* 13 (Summer):19–22.

Landes, William M., Lawrence Lessig, and Michael E. Solimine. 1998. "Judicial Influence: A Citation Analysis of Federal Courts of Appeals Judges." *Journal of Legal Studies* 27(June):271–332.

Landes, William M., and Richard A. Posner. 1976. "Legal Precedent: A Theoretical and Empirical Analysis." *Journal of Law and Economics* 19(August): 249–307.

Landis, Richard J., and Gary G. Koch. 1977. "The Measurement of Observer Agreement for Categorical Data." *Biometrics* 33(March):159–74.

Leiter, Brian. 1997. "Rethinking Legal Realism: Toward a Naturalized Jurisprudence." *Texas Law Review* 76(December):267–315.

Lemon v. Kurtzman. 1971. 403 U.S. 602.

Levi, Edward H. 1949. *An Introduction to Legal Reasoning*. Chicago: University of Chicago Press.

Lim, Youngsik. 2000. "An Empirical Analysis of Supreme Court Justices' Decision Making." *Journal of Legal Studies* 29(June):721–52.

Lloyd Corporation v. Tanner. 1972. 407 U.S. 551.

Long, J. Scott. 1997. *Regression Models for Categorical and Limited Dependent Variables.* Thousand Oaks, CA: SAGE Publications.

Maltz, Earl. 1988. "The Nature of Precedent." *North Carolina Law Review* 66(January):367–92.

Maltzman, Forrest, James F. Spriggs II, and Paul J. Wahlbeck. 2000. *Crafting Law on the Supreme Court: The Collegial Game.* New York: Cambridge University Press.

Maltzman, Forrest, and Paul J. Wahlbeck. 1996. "May It Please the Chief? Opinion Assignments in the Rehnquist Court." *American Journal of Political Science* 40(May):421–43.

Mapp v. Ohio. 1961. 367 U.S. 643.

Martin, Andrew. 2001. "Congressional Decision Making and the Separation of Powers." *American Political Science Review* 95(June):361–78.

Mathews v. Eldridge. 1976. 424 U.S. 319.

Mayflower Transit Co. v. Board of Railroad Commissioners. 1947. 332 U.S. 495.

McCune, David. 1995. "*United States v. Dixon*: What Does Same Offense Really Mean?" *Arkansas Law Review* 48(June):709–53.

McGuire, Kevin T., and Michael MacKuen. 2001. "A New Look at Stare Decisis: Citation Patterns on the U.S. Supreme Court." Presented at the Annual Meeting of the Midwest Political Science Association, Chicago, IL, April 19–22.

Merryman, John Henry. 1954. "The Authority of Authority: What the California Supreme Court Cited in 1950." *Stanford Law Review* 6(July):613–73.

———. 1977. "Toward a Theory of Citations: An Empirical Study of the Citation Practice of the California Supreme Court in 1950, 1960, and 1970." *Southern California Law Review* 50(March):381–428.

Minnick v. Mississippi. 1990. 498 U.S. 146.

Miranda v. Arizona. 1966. 384 U.S. 436.

Moe v. Confederated Salish and Kootenai Tribes of Flathead Reservation. 1976. 425 U.S. 463.

Mondak, Jeffery J. 1990. "Perceived Legitimacy of Supreme Court Decisions: Three Functions of Source Credibility." *Political Behavior* 12(December): 363–84.

———. 1994. "Policy Legitimacy and the Supreme Court: The Sources and Contexts of Legitimation." *Political Research Quarterly* 47(September):675–92.

Mondak, Jeffery J., and Shannon Ishiyama Smithey. 1997. "The Dynamics of Public Support for the Supreme Court." *Journal of Politics* 59(November): 1114–42.

Murphy, Walter F., James E. Fleming, and Sotirios A. Barber. 1995. *American Constitutional Interpretation.* 2nd ed. Westbury, NY: Foundation Press.

Murphy, Walter F., and C. Herman Pritchett. 1979. *Courts, Judges, and Politics: An Introduction to the Judicial Process.* New York: Random House.

Nalls, Charles H., and Paul R. Bardos. 1991. "Stare Decisis and the U.S. Court of International Trade: Two Case Studies of a Perennial Issue." *Fordham International Law Journal* 14(1):139–85.

Neal v. United States. 1996. 516 U.S. 284.

Nicholson, Stephen P., and Robert M. Howard. 2002. "Framing Support for the Supreme Court in the Aftermath of *Bush v. Gore.*" *Journal of Politics* 65 (August):676–95.

Pacelle, Richard L., and Lawrence Baum. 1992. "Supreme Court Authority in the Judiciary: A Study of Remands." *American Politics Quarterly* 29(April): 169–91.

Padden, Amy L. 1994. "Overruling Decisions in the Supreme Court: The Role of a Decision's Vote, Age, and Subject Matter in the Application of Stare Decisis after *Payne v. Tennessee.*" *Georgetown Law Journal* 82(April):1689–1732.

Payne v. Tennessee. 1991. 501 U.S. 808.

Peczenik, Aleksander. 1997. "The Binding Force of Precedent." In *Interpreting Precedents: A Comparative Study,* ed. D. Neil MacCormick and Robert S. Summers. Brookfield, VT: Ashgate Publishing.

Phelps, Glenn A., and John B. Gates. 1991. "The Myth of Jurisprudence: Interpretive Theory in the Constitutional Opinions of Justices Rehnquist and Brennan." *Santa Clara Law Review* 31(3):567–96.

Phillips, Scott, and Ryken Grattet. 2000. "Judicial Rhetoric, Meaning-Making, and the Institutionalization of Hate Crime Law." *Law & Society Review* 34(3): 567–606.

Planned Parenthood v. Casey. 1992. 505 U.S. 833.

Powell, Lewis F., Jr. 1990. "Stare Decisis and Judicial Restraint." *Washington and Lee Law Review* 47(Spring):281–90.

Priest, George, and Benjamin Klein. 1976. "The Selection of Disputes for Litigation." *Journal of Legal Studies* 13(January):1–55.

Pritchett, C. Herman. 1948. *The Roosevelt Court: A Study in Judicial Politics and Values, 1937–1947.* New York: MacMillan.

Rasmusen, Eric. 1994. "Judicial Legitimacy as a Repeated Game." *Journal of Law, Economics, & Organization* 10(April):63–83.

Rehnquist, James C. 1986. "The Power That Shall Be Vested in a Precedent: Stare Decisis, the Constitution, and the Supreme Court." *Boston University Law Review* 66(March):345–76.

Richards, Mark J., and Herbert M. Kritzer. 2002. "Jurisprudential Regimes in Supreme Court Decision Making." *American Political Science Review* 96(June): 305–20.

Rohde, David W. 1972. "Policy Goals, Strategic Choice, and Majority Opinion Assignments in the U.S. Supreme Court." *Midwest Journal of Political Science* 16(November):652–82.

Rohde, David W., and Harold J. Spaeth. 1976. *Supreme Court Decision Making.* San Francisco: W.H. Freeman.

Rosenberg, Gerald N. 1991. *The Hollow Hope: Can Courts Bring About Social Change?* Chicago: University of Chicago Press.

Rowland, C. K., and Robert A. Carp. 1996. *Politics and Judgment in the Federal District Courts.* Lawrence, KS: University Press of Kansas.

Scalia, Antonin. 1994. "The Dissenting Opinion." *Journal of Supreme Court History* 1994:33–44.

Schaefer, Walter V. 2004. "Precedent and Policy: Judicial Opinions and Decision Making." In *Judges on Judging: Views from the Bench*. 2nd ed. Ed. David M. O'Brien. Washington, DC: Congressional Quarterly Press.

Schauer, Frederick. 1987. "Precedent." *Stanford Law Review* 39(February): 571–605.

Schwartz, Bernard. 1996. *Decision: How the Supreme Court Decides Cases*. New York: Oxford University Press.

Scheb, John M., and William Lyons. 2001. "Judicial Behavior and Public Opinion: Popular Expectations Regarding the Factors that Influence Supreme Court Decisions." *Political Behavior* 32(June):181–94.

Schmidhauser, John R. 1962. "Stare Decisis, Dissent, and the Background of the Justices of the Supreme Court of the United States." *University of Toronto Law Journal* 14(2):194–212.

Segal, Jeffrey A. 1984. "Predicting Supreme Court Cases Probabilistically: The Search and Seizure Cases, 1962–1981." *American Political Science Review* 78(December):891–900.

———. 1985. "Measuring Change on the Supreme Court: Examining Alternative Models." *American Journal of Political Science* 29(August):461–79.

Segal, Jeffrey A., and Harold J. Spaeth. 1993. *The Supreme Court and the Attitudinal Model*. New York: Cambridge University Press.

———. 1996. "The Influence of *Stare Decisis* on the Votes of United States Supreme Court Justices." *American Journal of Political Science* 40(November): 971–1003.

———. 2002. *The Supreme Court and the Attitudinal Model Revisited*. New York: Cambridge University Press.

———. 2003. "Reply to the Critics of the Supreme Court Attitudinal Model Revisited." *Law and Courts Newsletter* 13(Summer):31–38.

Shapiro, Martin. 1965. "Stability and Change in Judicial Decision-Making: Incrementalism or Stare Decisis." *Law in Transition Quarterly* 2(Summer): 134–57.

Shapiro, Martin. 1972. "Toward a Theory of 'Stare Decisis.'" *Journal of Legal Studies* 1(January):125–34.

Shepard's Company. 1993. *Shepard's Citations In–House Training Manual*. Photocopy.

Smith v. Robbins. 2000. 528 U.S. 259.

Songer, Donald R. 1987. "The Impact of the Supreme Court on Trends in Economic Policy Making in the United States Courts of Appeals." *Journal of Politics* 49(August):830–41.

———. 1988. "Alternative Approaches to the Study of Judicial Impact: *Miranda* in Five State Courts." *American Politics Quarterly* 16(October):425–44.

Songer, Donald R., and Susan Haire. 1992. "Integrating Alternative Approaches to the Study of Judicial Voting: Obscenity Cases in the U.S. Courts of Appeals." *American Journal of Political Science* 36(November):963–82.

Songer, Donald R., and Stefanie A. Lindquist. 1996. "Not the Whole Story: The Impact of Justices' Values on Supreme Court Decision Making." *American Journal of Political Science* 40(November):1049–63.

Songer, Donald R., Jeffrey A. Segal, and Charles M. Cameron. 1994. "The Hierarchy of Justice: Testing a Principal-Agent Model of Supreme Court–Circuit Court Interactions." *American Journal of Political Science* 38(August): 673–96.

Songer, Donald R., and Reginald S. Sheehan. 1990. "Supreme Court Impact on Compliance and Outcomes: Miranda and New York Times in the United States Courts of Appeals." *Western Political Quarterly* 43(June):297–316.

Songer, Donald R., Reginald S. Sheehan, and Susan B. Haire. 2000. *Continuity and Change on the United States Courts of Appeals*. Ann Arbor, MI: University of Michigan Press.

Spaeth, Harold J. 1965. "Jurimetrics and Professor Mendelson: A Troubled Relationship." *Journal of Politics* 27(November):875–80.

———. 1995. *Expanded United States Supreme Court Judicial Database, 1946–1968 Terms. 1st Release*. Ann Arbor, MI: Inter-University Consortium for Political and Social Research.

———. 2001. *United States Supreme Court Judicial Database, 1953–2000 Terms*. Ann Arbor, MI: Inter-University Consortium for Political and Social Research.

Spaeth, Harold J., and Jeffrey A. Segal. 1999. *Majority Rule or Minority Will*. New York: Cambridge University Press.

Spinelli v. United States. 1969. 393 U.S. 410.

Spriggs, James F., II. 1996. "The Supreme Court and Federal Administrative Agencies: A Resource–Based Theory and Analysis of Judicial Impact." *American Journal of Political Science* 40(November):1122–51.

———. 1997. "Explaining Federal Bureaucratic Compliance with Supreme Court Opinions." *Political Research Quarterly* 50(September):567–93.

———. 2003. "The Attitudinal Model: An Explanation of Case Dispositions, Not Substantive Policy Outcomes." *Law and Courts Newsletter* 13(Summer): 23–26.

Spriggs, James F., II, and Thomas G. Hansford. 2000. "Measuring Legal Change: The Reliability and Validity of Shepard's Citations." *Political Research Quarterly* 53(June):327–41.

———. 2001. "Explaining the Overruling of U.S. Supreme Court Precedent." *Journal of Politics* 63(August): 1091–11.

———. 2002. "The U.S. Supreme Court's Incorporation and Interpretation of Precedent." *Law & Society Review* 36(1):139–60.

Stern, Nat. 1989. "State Action, Establishment Clause, and Defamation: Blueprints for Civil Liberties in the Rehnquist Court." *University of Cincinnati Law Review* 57(4):1175–242.

Stevens, John Paul. 1983. "The Life Span of a Judge-Made Rule." *New York University Law Review* 58(April):1–21.

Traut, Carol Ann, and Craig F. Emmert. 1998. "Expanding the Integrated Model of Judicial Decision Making: The California Justices and Capital Punishment." *Journal of Politics* 60(November):1166–80.

Tuan Anh Nguyen v. I.N.S. 2001. 533 U.S. 53.

Tushnet, Mark. 1988. *Red, White, and Blue: A Critical Analysis of Constitutional Law*. Cambridge, MA: Harvard University Press.

Tyler, Tom R. 1984. "The Role of Perceived Injustice in Defendants' Evaluations of Their Courtroom Experience." *Law & Society Review* 18(1):51–74.

———. 1990. *Why People Obey the Law*. New Haven, CT: Yale University Press.

Tyler, Tom R., and Gregory Mitchell. 1994. "Legitimacy and the Empowerment of Discretionary Legal Authority: The United States Supreme Court and Abortion Rights." *Duke Law Journal* 43(February):703–802.

Tyler, Tom R., and Kenneth Rasinski. 1991. "Procedural Justice, Institutional Legitimacy, and the Acceptance of Unpopular U.S. Supreme Court Decisions: A Reply to Gibson." *Law & Society Review* 25(3):621–29.

Ulmer, S. Sidney. 1959. "An Empirical Analysis of Selected Aspects of Lawmaking of the United States Supreme Court." *Journal of Public Law* 8(Fall): 414–36.

———. 1970. "Dissent Behavior and the Social Background of Supreme Court Justices." *Journal of Politics* 32(August):580–98.

Unger, Roberto. 1983. *The Critical Legal Studies Movement*. Cambridge, MA: Harvard University Press.

United States v. Bauer. 1947. 331 U.S. 532.

United States v. Bramblett, 1955. 348 U.S. 503.

United States v. Felix. 1992. 503 U.S. 378.

United States v. Morrison. 2000. 529 U.S. 598.

Van Hees, Martin, and Bernard Steunenberg. 2000. "The Choices Judges Make: Court Rulings, Personal Values, and Legal Constraints." *Journal of Theoretical Politics* 12(July):305–23.

Vasquez v. Hillery. 1986. 474 U.S. 254.

Vinson, Fred. M. 1949. "Work of the U.S. Supreme Court." *Texas Bar Journal* 12(December):551–52, 576–78.

Wahlbeck, Paul J. 1997. "The Life of the Law: Judicial Politics and Legal Change." *Journal of Politics* 59(August):778–802.

———. 1998. "The Development of a Legal Rule: The Federal Common Law of Public Nuisance." *Law & Society Review* 32(3):613–37.

Wahlbeck, Paul J., James. F. Spriggs II, and Forrest Maltzman. 1999. "The Politics of Dissents and Concurrences on the U.S. Supreme Court." *American Politics Quarterly* 27(October):488–514.

Wald, Patricia M. 1995. "The Rhetoric and the Results of Rhetoric: Judicial Writings." *University of Chicago Law Review* 62(Fall):1371–419.

Walsh, David J. 1997. "On the Meaning and Pattern of Legal Citations: Evidence from State Wrongful Discharge Precedent Cases." *Law & Society Review* 31(2):337–60.

Warren Trading Post v. Arizona Tax Commission. 1965. 380 U.S. 685.

Wechsler, Herbert. 1959. "Toward Neutral Principles of Constitutional Law." *Harvard Law Review* 73(November):1–35.

Weeks v. United States. 1914. 232 U.S. 383.

Westerland, Chad. 2003. "Who Owns the Majority Opinion? An Examination of Policy Making on the Supreme Court." Presented at the Annual Meeting of the American Political Science Association, Philadelphia, PA, August 28–31.

White, Halbert. 1980. "A Heteroskedasticity-Consistent Covariance Matrix Estimator and a Direct Test for Heteroskedasticity." *Econometrica* 48(May): 817–38.

White Mountain Apache Tribe v. Bracker. 1980. 448 U.S. 136.

Wolf v. Colorado. 1949. 338 U.S. 25.

Wood, B. Dan, and James E. Anderson. 1993. "The Politics of U.S. Antitrust Regulation." *American Journal of Political Science* 37(February):1–39.

Yates v. Evatt. 1991. 500 U.S. 391.

Index

abortion-related decisions, influences, 3, 10
Aero Mayflower Transit Co. v. Board of Railroad Commissioners, 81n3
agenda of court, as control variable, 41, 62, 82–83, 90, 98n6
age of precedent: and frequency of interpretation, 52–54, 116; and measurement of precedent vitality, 23–25, 60–61
age of precedent, as control variable: generally, 63, 126; lower court model, 120–21; negative interpretation model, 63, 73; overruling of precedent model, 83; positive interpretation model, 63, 73; treatment case model, 98, 106
Aguilar v. Texas, 78, 87–88
Aldisert, Rugero J., 23
Amalgamated Food Employees Union Local 590 v. Logan Valley Plaza, Inc., 1–2
American Trucking Assns., Inc. v. Scheiner, 81n3
amici filings, as control variable: generally, 62, 63n14, 80–81n; negative interpretation model, 62, 73; overruling of precedent model, 80–81n, 82–83, 90; positive interpretation model, 62, 73; treatment case model, 98, 99
Anders v. California, 55–56, 58, 73–74
Arizona Tax Commission, Warren Trading Post v., 6–8
assembly rights, 1–2
attitudinal model, 3–4, 9–11, 129–30, 132

Bauer, United States v., 94, 101
Benesh, Sara, 110
bivariate probit model, 58–59n4
Board of Railroad Commissioners, Aero Mayflower Transit Co. v., 81n3
Bracker, White Mountain Apache Tribe vs., 7
Bramblett, United States v., 81n3
breadth of precedent, as control variable, 62, 73, 82–83, 90, 98
breadth of treatment case, as control variable, 99, 106

Brennan, William J., 93, 103
Brenner, Saul, 10, 80–81
Bueno de Mesquita, Ethan, 24n6
Bush v. Gore, 26n8

California, Anders v., 55–56, 58, 73–74
Cameron, A. Colin, 115n11
Cardozo, Benjamin, 22
Casey, Planned Parenthood v., 21–22, 26–27
Central Hardware Co. v. National Labor Relations Board, 2
citation pattern research, 10n6
citations of precedent. *See* lower court model
coalitions. *See* concurring opinions, as control variable; majority opinions; margin of vote, as control variable
coding scheme, *Shepard's Citations,* 44–46, 50
concurring opinions, as control variable: generally, 41, 61, 126; lower court model, 120; negative interpretation model, 61, 72–73; overruling of precedent model, 82–83, 90; positive interpretation model, 61, 72–73; treatment case model, 98
Confederated Salish and Koonenai Tribes of Flathead Reservation, Moe v., 7
congressional overrides, as control variable, 62n13
constitutional precedent, as control variable, 62, 73, 82–83, 90–91, 98
control variables: generally, 41, 61–63, 80–81n; lower court model, 114, 120–21; negative interpretation model, 61–63, 72–73; overruling of precedent model, 80–81n, 82–83, 90–91; positive interpretation model, 61–63, 72–73; treatment case model, 98–99, 101n12, 105–6
Corbin, Grady v., 93–94, 103
court-appointed attorneys, 55–56
Cox proportional hazards model, 81–91